# ANOINTED
## TO HEAL

# ANOINTED
## TO HEAL

*True Stories and Practical Insight
for Praying for the Sick*

# RANDY CLARK
# AND BILL JOHNSON

**Chosen**

*a division of Baker Publishing Group*
Minneapolis, Minnesota

Published by Chosen Books
11400 Hampshire Avenue South
Bloomington, Minnesota 55438
www.chosenbooks.com

Chosen Books is a division of
Baker Publishing Group, Grand Rapids, Michigan

Previously published under the title *Healing Unplugged*

Printed in the United States of America

Library of Congress Cataloging-in-Publication Data
Names: Johnson, Bill, author. | Clark, Randy, author.
Title: Anointed to heal : true stories and practical insight for praying for the sick / Randy Clark and Bill Johnson.
Other titles: Healing unplugged
Description: Minneapolis, Minnesota : Chosen, a division of Baker Publishing Group, [2017] | Previously published as Healing unplugged / Bill Johnson and Randy Clark, 2012.
Identifiers: LCCN 2016036272 | ISBN 9780800798239 (trade paper : alk. paper)
Subjects: LCSH: Spiritual healing. | Healing—Religious aspects—Christianity. | Johnson, Bill—Interviews. | Clark, Randy—Interviews.
Classification: LCC BT732.5 .J593 2017 | DDC 234/.131—dc23
LC record available at https://lccn.loc.gov/2016036272

The internet addresses, email addresses, and phone numbers in this book are accurate at the time of publication. They are provided as a resource. Baker Publishing Group does not endorse them or vouch for their content or permanence.

Cover design by Dan Pitts

17  18  19  20  21  22  23        7  6  5  4  3  2  1

I dedicate my portion of this book to Cal and Michelle Pierce, who head up the International Association of Healing Rooms based in Spokane, Washington. They have paid a big price to bring healing to nations all over the world with both purity and power. I have been greatly impacted by their faith and devotion. I honor their efforts for the King and His Kingdom, and I am privileged to call them friends.

—Bill Johnson

I dedicate this book to all the students who have been part of our Global School of Supernatural Ministry, to the men and women who have served me as my interns or personal assistants and to the pastors and itinerant ministers of our Apostolic Network of Global Awakening. You have been part of my life and have challenged me to keep pressing in for more.

I also dedicate this book to my wife and children, who have shared me with the world, which is my parish.

—Randy Clark

# CONTENTS

# ACKNOWLEDGMENTS

I want to thank Randy Clark for the honor of his friendship. I also want to thank Jane Campbell of Chosen Books, along with her amazing staff, for serving both readers and authors well. I am in your debt.

—Bill Johnson

I want to thank Bill Johnson, my apostolic overseer and friend. Thank you for challenging me to step out of my comfort zone in regard to the ministry of healing. You have been such an encouragement to me.

I want to acknowledge Jane Campbell, who greatly encourages me and who believed in this book when I shared my idea for it. Also Trish Konieczny, whom I totally have enjoyed working with as an editor, and the whole staff of Chosen Books, who have exhibited such professionalism in their work. You are a great team to work with. Thanks for believing in Bill and me.

—Randy Clark

# INTRODUCTION

**From Bill Johnson:**

> As iron sharpens iron, so one man sharpens another.
>
> Proverbs 27:17

No one has had a greater influence on me as it pertains to the lifestyle of miracles, signs and wonders than Randy Clark. I have ministered with him all over the world and have been greatly impacted. His lifestyle and message have shaped my thinking and behavior. I have heard some of his messages more times than I can count, yet they never get old. In fact, I am challenged every single time he speaks. The standard he holds for his personal life, the way he honors people, and most of all, his commitment to honor and follow the Holy Spirit have inspired me beyond words. *Iron sharpens iron.* I have heard that concept taught many times in the church, but it is usually a description of how God can use our differences to improve one another's personalities and giftings. While that is true, I do not use it in that sense. My edge is sharper, my resolve is stronger and I am better in every

13

way because of Randy's patient instruction, both to me and to the people we serve.

This interview concept was Randy's idea. This kind of interaction is really my favorite way to learn and communicate truth. Initially it was not intended as a book, but instead as a potential DVD project to help train people (specifically his students) in this kind of ministry. The presence of God became so obvious and strong during these interview times, though, that we knew He was up to something more significant than we originally had planned.

The conversational nature of our interview project ensures that it remains practical and intensely honest. It was refreshing to be part of this. The text in these pages is taken directly from our interviews, though we have changed a word or phrase as needed to help the reader capture the intended message more accurately, since conversation does not always translate well into print. (We also have added a few parenthetical explanations where needed.)

Randy and I have partnered together for life and ministry in covenant friendship for the past fourteen years. I believe it is a God-ordained partnership where each of our strengths adds to the other's overall success in life. Iron truly sharpens iron, and it is a great blessing.

**From Randy Clark:**

This book is based on two interviews about the healing ministry. I interviewed Bill Johnson; I then had Bill interview me. Our two interviews are part of a set of twelve interviews that I conducted with people noted for healing. In addition to Bill and me, the interviews involved Dr. Heidi Baker, Dr. James Maloney, Ian Andrews, Todd White, Jim and Ramona Rickard, Leif Hetland, Cal Pierce, Henry Madava, Omar Cabrera and Carlos Annacondia. I did these interviews because I believe that people just starting out in the healing ministry or desiring to have a healing ministry could gain much from the wisdom of these men and women who have strong healing gifts. If the normal person interested in healing could interview these highly gifted men and women, what a great advantage it would be. This project was a way to give them that opportunity.

When I had the opportunity to interview famous healers, I usually asked them questions about the same five areas:

1. What is your story? How were you called into the healing ministry and what major events or experiences have been part of your call?
2. How have you grown in the area of healing and miracles, and what have you learned?
3. Have you experienced any breakthrough events that caused you to see an increase in healing?
4. How have you developed your ability to see and/or hear in the Spirit?
5. Would you share with me the four or five greatest stories of miraculous healings or deliverances you have experienced?

Since I was so interested in these questions, I believed many other people interested in healing would be, as well, and would learn from the answers these gifted people could offer. These are the basic questions Bill and I asked each other in our interviews, although we also covered some other interesting topics relating to healing along the way, as you will see.

Initially, I recorded these interviews to be used in the new Christian Healing Certification Program I was developing to offer online that would involve components for physical healing, inner healing (or soul care) and deliverance. But after Bill and I completed our interviews of each other, I was so excited about the content of the interviews that I contacted Jane Campbell of

Chosen Books and told her I believed these two interviews would make a great book. As you can see, she agreed. If this book is as well received and as helpful to those interested in healing as I think it will be, I have ten more interviews waiting. I will follow through with my main purpose by using these interviews in our online courses, and I believe I will also use them in our nine-month residency school in Mechanicsburg, Pennsylvania, the Global School of Supernatural Ministry. But my hope now is that these interviews also will turn into a valuable set of teaching tools in the form of books like this one.

I interviewed Bill at our Voice of the Apostles conference in October 2010, late one night between 11:30 P.M. and 1:30 A.M.—after a long evening at the conference. He needed to get up in three or four hours to fly home, but we felt as though the interview was so important that we needed to do it anyway. Our schedules were crazy with so many meetings that finding a time when we were together and had video equipment available was a challenge, but we did it. Bill interviewed me at my School of Healing and Impartation: Deliverance, Disbelief and Deception conference in Abilene, Texas, in November 2010. Again, it was late at night because it was the only time we could find. The Global School of Healing and Impartation conferences are packed with six lectures a day for four days, and I had meetings at each mealtime in Abilene. But we both believed the interview was so important that we had to do whatever was necessary to get it recorded. The book you hold is the result of our determined efforts.

Bill and I have known each other for about fourteen years. We have served each other in ministry, and we greatly respect each other. I have gone to Bill's church, Bethel, many times and have also spoken for him in his school, Bethel School of Supernatural Ministry, on which we patterned our Global Awakening nine-month residence school. Bill in turn has committed to serve me by speaking in about five of my schools or conferences per year. The Holy Spirit has truly drawn the two of us together. Early on, a prophetic minister looked at Bill and "saw" him turn into me. Another time, a prophetic minister saw Bill and me as joined at the hip. Another prophetic minister told Bill he believed God wanted us to work together on a book. And Bill's personal secretary believed that God showed her in the Spirit that Bill and I were to work together. I am excited that these interviews are one way we are doing that.

This book is a very close rendition of the interviews Bill and I conducted with each other. However, since verbal communication and written communication are so different in style, some editing was done to make for easier reading of our spoken words. Occasionally this book will differ from the videos in places where, on reading the actual interview transcripts, we caught a mistake. Those we corrected in this book version. Additionally, we added a few notes for the readers that clarify some of our spoken references in the interview process. I believe these notes add some important information and make some of our statements much more meaningful.

We made a careful effort, however, to keep the text of this book as close to our actual interviews as possible. The book and the recorded interviews therefore follow each other closely and could be used together easily to supplement each other. Having a written copy of this healing information on hand to study and refer back to will be valuable. So will watching a recorded version, in which you will feel as though you are right there with us, taking part in our conversation and getting to know us better. (These conversations were recorded in HD.) Both versions will give you a real-life glimpse into what taking part in a healing ministry involves and will show you how very powerfully the Spirit of God is working in healings today.

# PART 1

# RANDY CLARK
# INTERVIEWS
# BILL JOHNSON

# 1

# GOING AFTER HEALING

**Randy:** Tonight I'm interviewing Bill Johnson, a man who has greatly encouraged me in the ministry of healing. I know what Bill has to say tonight will greatly encourage all of you who are watching these interviews on DVD or reading about them in our book *Anointed to Heal*.

Bill, I want to thank you for taking the time out of your crazy schedule to take part in this interview, especially as late as it is right now. I think it's 11:30 at night here. We're in Baltimore, Maryland, for the Voice of the Apostles conference, and we just got out of a wonderful service with Heidi Baker. I know you're tired.

**Bill:** I'm glad to do this interview, Randy. I think it's important.

**Randy:** I know it's in your heart and my heart both to provide these next generations coming up with materials they can use to minister effectively. If they can learn from these interviews some of the spiritual principles that you and I learned by long experience, and sometimes by trial and error, they can minister to more people more effectively and more quickly.

To get started with this interview, Bill, the first thing I want to ask you about is your life story. How did it happen that you began to feel this call, this burden to pray for the sick? What did God do? Were there any experiences or circumstances you can think of that were connected to this call? Could you tell us about it?

**Bill:** I grew up in a home where we believed in healing; the practice at our church was to pray for the sick. I don't remember ever seeing anyone healed; it was more like we believed in it, so we did it. But I don't remember growing up with any expectation that something would happen. And we were usually too afraid to check people out after we prayed. When we did, we never saw anything.

Still, a belief that healing could happen was in my DNA. I grew up that way; my family history is very strong in that area. Even though healings didn't seem to be taking place when I was growing up, I remember hearing stories about healings that took place in a previous generation. That probably played a huge part in my life because it planted seeds in me. I knew healings hadn't just taken place two thousand years ago, or just overseas in Africa or Brazil or somewhere. I knew they had taken place here in the United States, even if they had happened years before.

And I just got hungry. You keep reading the gospels and you find that healing never leaves the gospels—it's always there, on every page. At some point you have to deal with it. You either have to turn a cold shoulder and think, *This is just not for me; it's not for this time.* Or else you're obligated to pursue healing and find out more about it. I wound up telling myself, *I may stink at this, but it's pretty clear that we're supposed to do it.*

22

I remember one of the real trigger points for me. Someone gave me some books from John G. Lake. Now you can get his books all together in one big volume that Roberts Liardon put together. But these were little booklets, and they messed me up huge because I read them and realized, *This is extreme.* And it put such an appetite in me that I just couldn't stand it. So I actually started taking time in services and trying words of knowledge. I didn't do it well, but I did the best I could, calling out whatever seemed to come to mind. Then we'd pray for people, and still nothing seemed to happen.

In 1987 I went to a couple of John Wimber conferences. One was specifically about healing, and the other was about something else. Something happened to me at those. I never received prayer; nobody ever prophesied "you'll have a healing anointing" over me or anything. I never had an experience like that. I just got dissatisfied that I was living a Gospel that didn't include healing, but Jesus modeled a different kind. And that just messed me up inside. I pastored for a while, pursuing healings in meetings and stuff, and still never saw anything happen. But we still went after healing because we believed it was right.

The healing conference was both wonderful and frustrating. It was wonderful because of what I saw happen. It was frustrating because it was the only time I'd ever been to a conference in my life where every single teaching I heard was something I had taught before. It was weird—they even used some of the same illustrations that I thought were mine! That has to be divinely orchestrated. It was frustrating because I had no evidence for what I believed. I had no fruit. I believed in healing, so I'd teach on it, but still nothing happened. Obviously it wasn't doctrine itself that was the problem. I came home from that conference with a conviction that I was obligated to seek fruit for what I believed.

It was not enough for me just to have good theology and even go through the motions of praying. I'd read something, I'd get really encouraged, we'd faithfully pray for people for a while, then, when nothing happened, we'd back off. Pretty soon I wasn't praying for anybody unless they asked. And then I'd read something else or I'd get stirred up out of the gospels, and I'd go after it again, but still nothing happened.

When I came back from that Wimber conference, I knew it was not an option—I couldn't back off ever again. Healing had to become a part of who we were. There were still seasons of ups and downs, but I realized that I was obligated to require fruit for what I believed. It's a hard thing to teach anybody about, because it's hard to describe what goes on inside of you. But there's almost this idea, *Wait a minute, I don't have to settle for fruitlessness.* And so you cry out to God in private and you take risks in public, and that was it. My first miracle was in a store. I knew the owner, so I went by to see him.

"Bill, I'm going to have to retire," the owner told me. He was only in his forties. He said, "I've got arthritis so badly I can't use my tools; I can't even take boxes off the shelves."

The store was full of people, so I didn't pray with him. Since I'd never seen anything happen, I wasn't real courageous about it. I did have that conviction in me, though, because I'd just gotten back from Wimber's deal. So I returned to the store the next day, and no customers were there. I was really thankful. The owner brought up his health issues again, and it was as if God was helping, shoving me over the edge.

I said, "Dave, I believe God wants to heal you. Could I pray for you?"

"Sure," he said.

I said, "Would you sit down?" I didn't know what to do, so I just put my hands on his elbows and his hands, and the best

I knew how, I asked God to heal him. I rebuked arthritis, and he started moving around. The guy was absolutely, stunningly healed. I was shocked! He was shocked!

This has been quite a few years ago, 23 years now, and he still talks to friends about that day Jesus healed him. At first he thought *I* was a great healer. When I came back to his store some weeks after he was healed, I asked him, "How are you doing?"

He replied, "You're a great healer."

You can't expect the world to have good theology, as messed up as we are ourselves sometimes, so I let him talk. Then I said, "David, thank you so much. I know you're trying to encourage me and compliment me, and I appreciate it, but what happened is the Holy Spirit gives these gifts that Jesus has to people, and He let me deliver one to you. And it was really because Jesus walked into the room."

The next time I saw him after that, he said, "Bill, you're a great—" and he stopped himself. "I was visited by Jesus," he said instead.

Dave's healing was a real breakthrough moment for us because I saw it could happen. And right after that, we started seeing more. I was so hungry for healing that one of the things I did was teach a class on healing. I figured, *I've got to do something here to create more momentum to get breakthrough.* We used Wimber's stuff and Mario Murillo's and Charles and Frances Hunter's. It was about as diverse a spectrum as you could possibly get. We'd use their material, and we'd copy them. If they did something, we'd do it right after them. The Hunters would hold out their arms, so we'd hold out our arms. Wimber would do his thing; Mario would call out words of knowledge. Literally, twenty of us in a room would watch these people on a video, then I'd say, "All right, let's do what they do." We'd get up and mimic them, and we started seeing breakthrough all through the church.

It was contagious because it never was just me. It started with everybody, all those people together in the class. That became a cell group that started spearheading things. It was wonderful, and it started because I saw it in the gospels but not in me, so I was trying to get something to ignite a fire in me. I didn't know how. I didn't know anything about impartation, so I read John G. Lake, and that ignited something in me. Then going to the Wimber conferences and seeing this stuff was actually working finally brought me hope that this could happen in my lifetime, that I could see fruit for what I believed.

**Randy:** Is there any significance that the way the first healing happened wasn't in church, it was with a lost person? Or was that just a fluke? After you came back from the conference, had you practiced by praying for people in church, yet still you saw nothing? I want to make sure I'm representing this correctly—that the first healing was a lost man outside of the church, not the first person you prayed for after you got back?

**Bill:** You've got it right. The first healing was the lost guy in a public place, not someone we prayed for in church.

**Randy:** Is there any significance to that, do you think, or was it just a random thing?

**Bill:** I think it was extremely significant, and it has had a tremendous effect on how we live now. Just a little background: The church *was* strong in worship, extremely strong. It was very healthy and also had developed a very strong prophetic culture. We were accustomed to seeing bizarre things happen out in public while praying with somebody or ministering to somebody. When the miracle happened, that was a crowning touch. We knew this stuff had to be taken outside of the church.

I think it was a setup by the Lord. In fact, I have no question about it because seeing that happen planted in me a priority focus on getting it outside the church. And *then* we started seeing it in the church.

**Randy:** You must have been so excited. This was at Weaverville, up in the mountains, correct?

**Bill:** Yes, Weaverville. I had been there for nine years by this time. Pastoring, going up and down about praying for the sick—trying to go after it, getting discouraged, going after it, getting discouraged. So finally there was this beginning! I just couldn't believe it. I remember praying for another guy on the street who walked with a major limp and watching God touch him. And praying for a relative of his in a hospital who just had this encounter with God. We just started going for it. It was wonderful.

**Randy:** After you personally got the breakthrough, did it start in others quickly, too?

**Bill:** As I said, we had that class of about twenty people, so we were all learning the same stuff. We all realized we didn't know anything, so we watched those videos and copied them. Then we'd take it from the class into the church and do the same thing.

One guy had a serious back injury. He couldn't bend over, pick up a chair or anything. He was a big weightlifter guy totally out of commission. He was permanently laid up and in a lot of pain. After our class started, there was such a momentum that the cell group leader called him up and said, "Don, you need to come this week. You're going to get healed."

Don came and got healed. The next day, he split two cords of wood. If you've ever done that, you know that will kill a good back!

That momentum started hitting in the church. Let me add that when we came back from the Wimber conference and started praying for people in the church, they had started falling, too. We hadn't seen that before—that is, I had seen it, but it hadn't happened when I prayed for people. We started seeing that, too, so there was enthusiasm in the room just because we knew God was doing things.

**Randy:** To follow up on what you said, before you went down to see Wimber in Anaheim, as a pastor, you hadn't yet seen people in your church in Weaverville fall. You came back to your church, and they started falling when you prayed, right? You didn't talk about falling, right, so no one could say it was the power of suggestion—it was just a new thing? Do you think there was some type of anointing just from being in Wimber's service?

**Bill:** There had to be. We were different when we came back. And there was no impartation prayer at the conference. When I teach on impartation now, I talk about the importance of the laying on of hands, but there's something you can get in a room without that if you learn how to receive the grace that's being ministered. There are several ways to receive an impartation; in community you can receive it. That happened to us. We didn't know anything, not even the concept of impartation. But when we got back, stuff was happening that none of us had ever seen before in our ministry. In fact, the church I was pastoring contained the most spiritually *ungifted* group of people when I arrived in 1978. It was much different at that time. They were wonderful, loving people, but had no gifts of the Spirit at all. So it was an uphill battle, but we were gain- ing momentum. The prophetic was strong, and in worship we learned things were in the anointing, in the presence of God.

When people started falling, losing their balance, we thought, *Wow, we've never seen this before!* And it happened with all of us who had been down there at Wimber's; we just picked something up.

**Randy:** That's exciting. It sounds as though there are some parallels in our lives, yours and mine—a lot more than I realized!

# 2

# GROWTH SPURTS IN HEALING

**Randy:** The second question I want to ask you, Bill, is about your massive growth personally. I first came to your church around 1998, so we've known each other for over a decade. I've seen you grow tremendously in that time, which has been a great encouragement to me. What do you think has caused this growth? Is there anything in particular you've learned about healing because you've grown in that area? And some of your growth, in my opinion, is not just an increase in anointing or gifting; it's a greater understanding about how to cooperate with God. Could you speak to that?

**Bill:** It started in 1987 when we went to the Wimber conference, but we lost a lot of what we gained in a short amount of time because I didn't know how to maintain the fire. I was convinced that God would use all of us in healing; I had no question about that. Yet we lost some of our sense of the presence and power of God. I could look back to Anaheim and see that something had happened there even though nobody had prayed for me. I never got in any line; I was just there watching. On my way to Toronto in 1995, I said to the Lord, "God, if you'll touch me again the way You did then, I will never change the subject." (In these interviews, references to "Toronto" mean the church in Toronto, Canada, that experienced a great outpouring of the Holy Spirit that started in January 1994 when Randy went to do a four-day meeting there at the request of Pastors John and Carol Arnott. These meetings continued six nights a week for over twelve years. Now referred to as the "Toronto Blessing," that outpouring is considered one of the greatest revivals of the twentieth century.)

What I meant by changing the subject was that in hindsight, I could see that I had dropped the ball. I had allowed myself to become shaped by what didn't happen instead of motivated by what did. So I made a covenant with the Lord, I believe it was on the plane. I promised, "I will never change the subject if You'll touch me again."

In Toronto, I went up for prayer every time. They could have had a fake altar call and I'd have gone forward—I got prayer every time it was possible. I was really impacted, though I didn't have any unique experiences. But I stood in the lines with everybody else for the laying on of hands. And I came home knowing I had just seen what I wanted to see. God touched me, and a peace came on me. It was nothing dramatic, but it was still wonderful—just His glorious presence. I told Him, "All right, that's it. You've got the rest of my life. I will never change the subject again!"

That was the real beginning, because I came home and never one minute from that moment in 1995 to this, have I ever even deviated from what God has called me to do, from what He's given *us* to do. We started seeing stuff happen in the church again. It was gradual; it started in February and in about March or April, we had a sizable breakthrough. In August we had an unusual breakthrough. We had a service where the presence was so strong that I was afraid to talk. God was doing stuff all over the room. I knew I could mess it up, and all I had permission to do was occasionally give a direction—that was it. It was a breakthrough moment.

In October of that year, the Spirit of God fell with power in our church, like in Toronto. Bodies were everywhere, and we experienced a sustainable outpouring. The seed had been planted in February, but we reached a measure of maturity, or a birthing of it, in October. From that point on, there was no stopping it whatsoever. We had a continuous outpouring of the Spirit. We kept pastoring it. You know the verse where it talks about God lighting the fire on the altar, and it's the priests who keep it burning? (See Leviticus 6:12–13.) While I wasn't aware of the concept then, I had embraced the lifestyle, because I knew it was up to me now to keep the fire burning by continually putting sacrifices on the altar. (By sacrifices, in this context, I'm referring to making ourselves a living offering to God, with a willingness to do whatever He asks of us.)

The next February following that October, I became the pastor of Bethel Church in Redding, California. I came with a commission to bring revival there, and it started immediately on a Sunday night. I invited everyone to the front, and I invited the Spirit of God to come. Out of hundreds at the altar, the Spirit fell on one woman. I looked at Beni, my wife, she looked at me, and we said, "We've got it. It's now unstoppable."

We knew we just needed that crack in the dike, and that's how it happened. From that point on, it exploded. We started sovereignly having healings. People would come up and say, "My tumor's gone!" (I'm making a distinction here between

*'sovereign healings*

"sovereign healings" and the kind we see in the ministry of healing. Sovereign healings happen without our involvement—in the atmosphere of God's manifest presence, miracles happen. The ministry of healing is somewhat more dependent on us—we may give a word of knowledge, lay hands on the sick or even make a prophetic decree over them that releases the miracle for their bodies.)

About that time, in 1997, I flew out to see you in St. Louis. Rick Stivers set up an appointment for me to sit down with you. You were able to give us fifteen minutes during a really busy conference schedule.

**Randy:** I can actually picture that meeting! I remember going to a table, kneeling down beside it and talking to you guys.

**Bill:** Previous to that, we had just had six cases in eight weeks where either cancer was healed or tumors were disappearing. I was talking to Rick about that and said, "I really want to meet Randy."

Rick told me he would try to set it up, so he called you and was able to get us a little time. I flew to St. Louis, we attended a conference and I got fifteen minutes with you at the table. You were having a meeting right after you cut out fifteen minutes for us. I told you what we were seeing happen in Redding. You said you'd come, and you did come four or five months later. That's when we got the huge breakthrough. We were having a healing happen every week, maybe every two weeks. We were having people touched by God, which was wonderful. We saw deliverances and all kinds of stuff. But when you came, it went from weekly to daily. If you add up the numbers, almost hourly! It exploded. In the four days you were with us, we had over 400 people healed. In one meeting alone, the number was 129 or something. That was the most you had seen in North America in one place in one service.

In that release, that explosion, something happened to us. I know that you prayed over us and laid hands on us, and I know something happened in the environment where the whole church got it—we just got it. And we brought you back six months or a year after that, and it was like hammering that same nail. But that first four-day visit deposited something into us. It wasn't put on us; it was put *into* us. We already had the momentum, but when you came, it was like pouring gasoline on a fire. You came and imparted something to us that just exploded. And it's never gone back to what it was. It's never gone back.

**Randy:** Out of all the places I've gone, Bill, I can only think of three churches where that kind of thing happened. Your church was the first one, Henry Madava's church in the Ukraine was the second and Tom Jones's church was the third. Those three churches received a corporate anointing that transcended anything they'd experienced before, and they never went back. It was a sovereign thing, too, because I was teaching the same thing I taught at other churches I visited. In those three places, however, it was as if there was something that was in the mix. I believe it was the hunger and desire in the pastors and in the key leaders. I think it was also the sovereign election of God. Not to take away from human responsibility for the proper response and taking initiative—we're responsible to cooperate. But there's still something where sometimes God looks down and says, "I'm going to use that." And then He begins to orchestrate things to get a person ready. I believe for you and for Henry and Tom, and also in my own life, there was that sovereign side.

**Bill:** You're right. Cal Pierce was with us during that time. He was the "bored board member" who was planning an exit strategy to get out of the church. He'd been there 25 years, and he did not like what was happening. As a result of the beginning of this revival, though, I called a meeting with the elders. Cal came, still planning to leave the church. I invited the Spirit of God to come, and God chose him. The sovereign choice, you know! And now Cal is doing the whole healing room thing that is worldwide. It came out of this time and out of God's sovereign choice. I saw God possess a man—I've never seen it like that before or since. That sovereign choice thing is a big deal.

**Randy:** I know Wimber taught us, "When you're starting a church, pay attention to the people who get these very powerful visitations, because God is probably going to use them. You just pay attention."

Of course, you and I both know there's a big difference between someone getting a sovereign visitation and someone kind of mimicking someone else whom they saw get a visitation. So you've got to discern whether it's God or it's just good effort in the flesh. . . .

Tell us more about how you've grown and the things you've learned.

**Bill:** A key verse that really exploded for us during this time was that Jesus only did what He saw His Father do, only said what He heard His Father say. (See John 8:28–29.) Yet Jesus ministered to the woman who touched His garment and to the Syrophoenician woman who came to Him. He wasn't prepared to minister to them, but when He saw their faith, He did. That tells me that one of the ways Jesus learned what the Father was doing was by observing the response of the people who came to Him. That was part of how He recognized the Father was moving. Obviously I want to hear and be directed by the Lord, but I realize He's not going to give me everything directly. The Father didn't even do that to Jesus. Some of it was directed by the hunger, the draw, the faith of the people. Jesus saw something in that and realized, *The Father is in this*. Part of this process for me is learning how to recognize the Spirit of God working in someone, how to hear what God is saying and how to recognize faith in an individual.

I remember this gal came to me and said, "Tonight's my night."

I know you've had a thousand people say that to you, Randy, just as they've said it to me, and I always want to agree with them. But this one was different. When she walked up to me, I physically *felt* her faith. I don't know how to describe it. It so shocked me that I stepped back from her and tried to observe what was on her. You know Hebrews 5:14, where it talks about having your senses trained to discern good and evil? I was so overwhelmed by her faith that I looked at her not only with my eyes, but with all my senses. I looked at her head to toe and back up again because I never wanted to forget what I saw. I didn't know if I'd see anything with my eyes, but I thought I could get impacted somehow, it was so overwhelming to me.

She told me about her condition. She had a machine that pumped fluids into her heart. She could live only *four minutes* without the medication the fluids contained. Every morning at 7:00, she changed the bag. She asked, "Would you pray for me?"

I laid hands on her, and she went to the ground. Twenty minutes later she got up, and I asked, "How are you?"

She said, "There's a fire in my chest."

I said, "Your faith got you this one."

She left to drive home, which was a couple hours away. She showed up the next night at our meeting with half her church. She testified, "When I got up this morning, I went to change the bag of medication and the Lord said, 'You don't need it anymore.' So I removed it."

When you've got four minutes to find out whether you heard from God or not, you know that's faith! And the Lord healed her. Learning to see faith in someone else is a big deal. The apostle Paul saw that; he saw that the lame man in Acts 14 had the faith to be healed (see verses 8–9). I want to see that better. That's one of the things I'm working on. Wimber was so good at this, and you're amazing, looking around a crowd and seeing where the Spirit of God is touching people, seeing beyond the obvious manifestations. I'm getting breakthrough there in measure.

Another way God works with me is through inspired thought. Randy, you have words of knowledge that you feel a lot, and there's a certain severity that comes, which really is amazing to me. (Meaning there's an intensity to what you feel in your own body that shows you what God is healing, and the more intense it is, the more people will be healed or the more urgently the miracle is needed. That's my observation with you.) I can see when it happens, and I can tell there will be several people with that condition. And I do have that happen occasionally, but it's not the most frequent thing. For me, I have inspired thought. Or I'll see a word, though that's not often. I remember once when chaos was going on all over the room—ministry the way we like it, all over. I looked to my left to see what was happening, and I saw the word *tumor*. And literally, the second I saw it, I said, "Tumors." Tumors left five people's bodies with just that one sweep.

I've found out through delayed obedience—which is disobedience—that the longer you wait, the less anointing there is when you finally do obey. I don't want to make that a rule, but that's what's happened to me. When I've delayed on something, then I've finally given in and done it, it's not real powerful. So I've been trying to learn, if it's appropriate in that moment, to act within the second. And God showed me something in that moment when I said the word *tumors*, because five people had tumors that just disappeared. Just in an instance—nobody prayed for them—it was just as fast as the snap of the fingers, the wave of the hand. But it was when I saw the word, so I'm learning quick obedience.

Another thing, one of the most exciting things for me personally, is to see people healed without prayer. The first time this happened with me, at least en masse, was in Sydney, Australia. (I had one or two single instances happen before that.) I didn't have a ministry team with me that time; I was on my own. It was my first time at this church, and I wrote down ten or twelve words of knowledge ahead of time. I called out the first one, something to do with a knee. When I looked at the guy who responded, he just *looked* different. I can't tell you how—there wasn't a glow over him or anything. He just looked different, so I told him, "Stand up. Check it out."

He did, and right away he said, "It's healed!"

**Randy:** This is where you've helped me so much, Bill. Watching you, I've stepped into that now. But I wouldn't have done so if I hadn't seen you do it and had you speak to me about it and encourage me.

**Bill:** I can see an anointing for that is on you. What you carry is so powerful. And the whole thing is amazing. After the first guy, I thought, *I'll just go through and call out the other nine or ten words that I have, then we'll pray for them.* That's what I was going to do, call out all these words and turn people loose. And I called the second one; it was an injury in the eye, I think. I looked at the lady who raised her hand, and I can't tell you to this day what it was, but she stood out differently than anyone else in the room. I told her, "Stand up."

I've found that if you can get people to *do* something—it doesn't have to be noble—just get them to stand up or move into the aisle, action releases faith. If somebody has carpal tunnel, for example, I'll say, "Hold your hand up for thirty seconds." Faith needs an activity.

So I looked at this lady, and she just looked different. She stood out in the crowd. And I said, "Check out your eye." I went through all ten or twelve words of knowledge, and every single one of them got healed that way. Nobody prayed for them.

Another thing I started seeing happening at that meeting was that I'd call out a condition and several people would have it. Now, if someone has a broken ankle, for example, I'm not going to tell them to run on it out of the principle of faith. I won't do that—you can't put someone at risk out of a principle. But you may be required to put them at risk out of the presence of God. So I would call out and say, "Someone has a broken right ankle, and the Lord wants to heal that." Three people would raise their hands. I'd look, and one of them would stand out. Not all three; never all three. One. And I'd say to that person, "You should be healed. Get in the aisle and check it out." And the person would be healed. (I believe God displays His love and power in this way to increase the faith of others in the room, especially those who stand with the same need. After one person is healed without prayer, the others are much more inclined to believe God for their miracle when we pray for them, which we do quickly.)

I've even grabbed people's hands in situations like that and said, "Run!" And I won't give them an option; I just grab their hands. But only, *only* in recognition of the presence of God. I will never repeat that kind of thing just because it worked once—you could hurt someone. But I've been learning to recognize the presence that comes when the power of the Lord is present to heal. That's been exciting and so encouraging.

**Randy:** When you recognize the presence of God to heal a person, how does that work? Is it either/or? Either you see something different or have an impression when you look at a person? As you put it, the person *looks* different to you? Or does it sometimes happen that you don't really see anything different in the person, but something is happening in you? Or is it both/and?

**Bill:** It can be either/or. Sometimes it's both/and. Sometimes I call it the presence, but afterward, I look back and realize, *God gave me a gift of faith for that moment.* I think oftentimes, the presence actually comes with that gift—I both sense that presence and I operate out of that presence. And you know what it's like, Randy. In those moments, you just know what to do. It's as if I don't have time to think about it, and I better hurry and act or I'm going to deplete whatever's there. So I just know what to do, and I grab the person's hand and run, or I'll say, "Run!" Or I'll say, "Get into the aisle. All right, now jump!" Or whatever it might be. You just have a conviction about what to do. Faith is the conviction. So I try to pay attention to anything that just came up that I have a conviction about, and I identify a direction to go in.

I had a gal approach me who was missing a part of a leg muscle. She had heard me give a testimony about a miracle that took place when I was at Mahesh and Bonnie Chavda's tent meeting there in Charlotte. And this gal said, "I'm missing that same muscle you were talking about." And I was going to tell her I'd pray for her at the end of the meeting, then she said, "And I'm from Minnesota."

Well, Minnesota is where that miracle of new muscle being created started in the first place, and we've had it happen now so many times. Those two things about her triggered something, and I thought, *That's enough. That's the language of the Spirit, those two things. It's an unusual coincidence.* I told her, "Go to the back of the tent, then come and see me." (Sometimes the language of the Spirit includes unusual coincidences. When she said "Minnesota," I realized God wanted to heal her immediately instead of at the end of the meeting. The reason her answer stood out to me was the fact that the original creative miracle with that missing muscle started in Minnesota. The "coincidence" was enough to ignite faith in me for "right now.")

So she kind of jogged to the back of the tent, and by the time she got back up to me, her muscle had grown back. It came out of kind of a trigger where I could see that the Lord wasn't just doing it because it's what He does. It was more than that; He highlighted something unusual. It was a demonstration in front of the people.

So sometimes I know the presence is here even though I don't see anything different on a person. I didn't see anything different in that gal. Something triggered in *me*. But other times, it wasn't anything in me. It wasn't a conviction, it wasn't a gift of faith, it wasn't anything. When I looked at the person, however, he or she would stand out to me and I wouldn't know what it was about the person exactly, but I wouldn't take a long time to think about it. Four people would raise their hands with a condition, yet only one would stand out like that. The person would be highlighted somehow—not because there'd be a light or some unusual manifestation on the person. I've never stopped to figure it out, but it's probably just the Lord highlighting something, and maybe just to me, but not to anyone else in the room.

**Randy:** Are there any other things you've learned that have been particularly helpful for your growth in healing?

**Bill:** Following your model is always good. I've watched the way you pray for people and dialogue with them constantly and follow the anointing. I remember praying for a guy who had two bad knees. I think he needed knee replacements in both of them. I chose a side and started praying. I was praying for his right knee, and I asked, "Is anything happening?"

"Yeah," he said, "my left knee is on fire."

I thought, *All right, I'll go pray for the left knee!*

Getting feedback from people and learning to follow the anointing they're feeling is important. What I sense isn't always reliable for giving me direction. I can be having my own experience in God that's real, but it may not necessarily contribute to my getting a breakthrough for them. So learning from the way I've seen you dialogue with people to find out what they're experiencing, Randy, has been a huge thing for me. We've been together so many times now, in the ministry schools, in Brazil and all over the world. I've watched you, and it's been a tremendous help to me. Now I know better how to sense the anointing. I love when I sense the anointing. Certain things happen to me physically where I can tell that God is about to do something.

**Randy:** Do you want to elaborate on that for us? I think it will help others who are learning.

**Bill:** Okay. There's one thing I hardly ever refer to, but I'll do it in the context of this interview. I think it's probably time. One of the things that happens a lot is that I get this fire in my left hand. In intense times, it's in both hands, and it will even burn up my neck and up my chin. I've actually had times where it's very uncomfortable, it's such a heat. I won't ever ask the Lord to stop it; it's not that kind of thing. But it's not pleasant, if that makes sense. And I can tell there are times when that anointing will come and I can feel it especially strongly. I'll be in a certain setting where all of a sudden, it's like a silver dollar has been lying out in the hot summer sun for a while and somebody puts it in the palm of my hand. It's that kind of heat. And when that starts, I can tell there's an anointing present for healing. That just happened over time. It actually started early in the renewal. I didn't know it was connected to anything—I just thought it was connected to the Holy Spirit's presence. But since then, I've connected the dots. I've learned that it can happen when an anointing is present for healing or impartation.

Another thing happens to me that I don't talk about too often. I'll actually have this presence that comes on me. It's like a fire, and it will rest right over my right shoulder. It burns the side of my face. It's very funny looking back at when it started, because I didn't know what was going on. At first, I figured it might be when an angel was standing off to my side or something. I remember sitting at a banquet once where someone was up speaking. And this fire just started falling on me. I would lean my chin into it, then I'd pull my head back, then lean my chin into it . . . I was fascinated. It wasn't on the left; it was just on my right shoulder. So I kept leaning my chin into it and thinking, *Man, that's weird.*

After the banquet, the people sitting behind me said, "Could we massage your neck or do anything for you? We could see that you have a problem with your neck."

I started laughing because they had seen me move my head to the side repeatedly. So I finally said, "Oh, I'm sorry. My neck is fine. I was just experimenting with something." I didn't know what else to say.

Sometimes it happened when I would be traveling down the road with my team in the car. I'd be sitting in the passenger seat, the pastor would be driving and there'd be a couple people in the backseat. I'd go, "Oh, it just happened again." I'd put my hand there, and I could feel it. I didn't want to freak the pastor out since he was driving, but I'd tell the people in the back,

"Put your hand here." They would, and there would be that fire there. I didn't know what it was for probably two or three years.

**Randy:** When did it start, approximately? What year?

**Bill:** Probably 1998 or 1999. I remember it happening on a trip to Georgia when I did a conference with Ruth Heflin. I remember I'd get in certain environments and these things would start happening to me physically. The subject came up once when I was with Bob Jones. I don't remember how it came up because I wasn't telling anyone about this, but somehow it did. And I said, "I've got this fire that just gets on my shoulder. I figure it's an angel standing by me or something."

Bob said, "No, that's the Spirit that remains. Whenever He manifests, you'll notice it. It's on your right shoulder, so it has to do with authority. He's preparing you because you're going to have to do something that will take courage, and you'll have to use authority."

That connected! I could have explored what was happening for another twenty years and not come up with an answer like that. He put me on the fast track to realize and recognize when the Spirit of God is starting to manifest. I can sit on a plane and it will happen. I can be in a car on the way to an airport and it will happen. It might happen in my motel room. And I'll realize, *This trip is about courage. I've got to look for the moment when something needs to break loose and I'll need to be courageous or take authority.* Wherever or whenever it takes place, I'll know that God is calling me to the forefront for something. He gives me a little warning. Not always, but fairly often. That's how He happens to work with me.

**Randy:** That's really interesting and helpful. Do you want to fill us in on anything else you've learned?

**Bill:** I don't know if this will be helpful, and I don't have any of this down myself yet. But I've been learning on the one hand to go slow and take time with people. On the other hand, I've been learning to go fast. I know it's a strange combination.

I've watched you at this for years, Randy. When it comes to taking time, sometimes you'll spend your whole evening on *here* trying to get a breakthrough. More than anyone I know, you have the grace to pray long when you're supposed to. You have a grace to know when to do that. Every time I'm with you, I go home thinking, *I've got to learn this better.* And I work to improve, and I do improve.

**Randy:** I don't pray long as a normal thing. I cannot do it unless I know, *If I do this, it will come, this breakthrough.* I have faith for it. If I don't have faith for it, I can't pray like that.

**Bill:** I've come to realize that's true. I've tried it when I didn't have faith for it, and it wasn't working. But at times I've also honored the fact that God is working and I pay attention to what He's doing, not to what's not happening. So I stay there for an extended period of time. It's been wonderful to learn to do that.

I've also learned, however, that sometimes it's a waste for me to go long and I need to go quickly. It's not that people necessarily have evil intentions of stealing time—some do, but that's not a big deal. But there are some times where I've watched in meetings, and they pray long only because they don't believe God did anything. They actually pray past the miracle.

One of the first miracles we saw in Weaverville after the store owner was in our own group. This guy had horrible back issues, and I said, "Stand up and go over to the corner, and I'll get a group of people to pray for you." And as he was walking, I said, "Holy Spirit, come," and it about knocked him to the ground. I didn't have the courage to find out if he was healed, so I sent people over to pray for him. I went over, too, and prayed for about everything I could think of, because I still wasn't used to seeing anything happen.

When we were finally through, the guy said, "Oh yeah, I was healed after I got out of the chair and the Holy Spirit about knocked me down."

I've played with this a little bit. There are times when I'll turn people loose to pray, and I'll say, "Okay, lay hands on them and start to command." Then I'll say, "Okay, that's enough." I'll actually do it that fast, and they'll be shocked at how many people will already be healed. Randy, you can do it where people are just standing there with nobody praying for them. It's another sovereign way of healing that I think you have an unusual grace for. I do it now and then and it's wonderful, but I never see it happen the way I do when I watch you. You have this kind of an impartation in the room. Something happens when you release something over a crowd of people, and many will get healed. I'll have it, too, and I'll push into it, but it's mostly with you. But with the short prayer, I do see a lot of healings.

We've had bizarre things happen. In one of our current cell groups at Bethel, we've seen a lot of Hepatitis C healed. An individual came in and said, "I've just been diagnosed, I have Hepatitis C."

The cell group leader, who was walking past him to get a cup of coffee, kind of hit him on the arm and said, "Well, then, be healed." That's all he did.

The man went to the doctor, and the doctor confirmed that he didn't have it anymore. Yet it's medically impossible for it to be removed from your bloodstream. (That is, medical people have told me that Hepatitis C "scars" the blood in some way forever and you can't remove those indicators.) So that's another thing, learning when to move with God because He's moving fast.

**Randy:** So that's one of those accidental healings that you sometimes talk about? The cell group leader maybe wasn't even expecting it and maybe facetiously said "Be healed" as he walked past?

**Bill:** I think the leader who said it did expect it. But the person who had Hepatitis C was probably expecting some sort of a prayer. But I know the leader, and I think he just expected that he could give the command and it would be done, so he went on to get his coffee. It was amazing. Those are all probably kind of wrapped up in the same kind of lessons.

**Randy:** I probably need to get to our next question, but I'm laughing because I'm loving this. I'm actually learning as I'm talking with you. I think it would have been so exciting if you and I could have had videos like this to watch of the people who've gone ahead of us in this area. If they could have been talking like this, it would have been so helpful to us. It would have speeded up our growth curve.

**Bill:** It could have saved years because you and I have learned by experimenting. It's the joke around our place that Bethel is just an experiment. We try, we fail, we succeed—but we try. Seeing this kind of interview would have helped us a bunch.

# 3

# OPERATING IN THE UNUSUAL

**Randy:** The next question I want to ask, Bill, is about how you handle unusual instances. Are there certain times that you have a much stronger faith than usual that something is going to happen? For example, out of a group of words of knowledge, do you ever know a certain word is "the one," so you handle it differently? Do you ever kind of showcase that one for the people to see, to build faith? If that kind of unusual instance does happen, how does it happen for you? How do you handle it?

**Bill:** It happens two different ways I can think of offhand. The most unusual way—actually the most normal way, but maybe across the board with the people we work with, it might be the most unusual—is that it won't be a word of knowledge. It actually will be something that I've been seeing God do a lot. So I operate out of the concept of the testimony. I don't try to teach it, I don't mention it, I don't do anything. I just come.

Sometimes I'm lacking words of knowledge and lacking direction, so I'll start with whatever I saw God do last.

For example, just recently we've had this string of amazing miracles with head trauma. So now I can go into a meeting and I'll just call out head trauma, knowing that in most cases healings will happen. And I can tell that once we get going in it, God is going to display something in this one situation.

I've seen you do this, Randy, where you call it "one condition." That kind of breakthrough releases such faith that then you can go through the words of knowledge you have and turn everybody loose. That's what I'll see happen. I'll call out one condition: head trauma. Or for me, through the years, it's been people in automobile accidents. (At least, it started with automobile accidents. But it quickly expanded to accidents of any kind—sport injuries, falling off a ladder, any type of accident. Now they all are included in this prayer direction.) It's really a crazy thing, because it can be any part of the body that's injured. They'll have some sort of injury that's been there for twenty years, thirty years, the oldest one was seventy-two years. A woman was dropped on her tailbone as an infant, seventy-two years old, and the Lord healed her. I'll call out a condition and there'll be a certain anointing in the room, and you can see the Lord is going to demonstrate something.

I saw this thing on A. A. Allen's face once in a video of his that I watched. It was much more on him than I've ever experienced, but it makes me feel somewhat similar. He was walking around the cot of this woman who couldn't walk. He was walking around, to be honest, almost as if he were mocking sickness and mocking the devil, because he knew that in a moment something would happen, so he would just wait. Walk around and wait. He had that look on his face like, *This is going to happen!* There wasn't a question mark on his face. It's so stunning to me to see somebody's face like that.

Sometimes meetings will start, and you can tell when there's that presence there. You can tell, *The Lord's in charge of this one. I'm not having to prime the pump on this one. I'm not having to motivate or encourage; this is a God moment.* And when that happens, there's a breakthrough. I've seen it where there will be a specific miracle. It may come through a word of knowledge, but I would say probably two out of three times, it happens out of a testimony of what I've seen God do recently, where I've already seen the momentum. What happens is that I don't need a word of knowledge anymore in certain areas, because we have a history. I have ownership of a realm, in a sense.

**Randy:** It was a year ago that you told me about the metal disappearing, and I just went for it. I've never had a word of knowledge—not one about metal. I just went for it, and it has been the most amazing area of breakthrough. It didn't happen the first time, but then the Lord set me up the second time. But it's never been through a word of knowledge. It's like God set me up after that first time, and then we'd have numbers like 23 out of 47 getting healed. I just feel I'm to go for it in this area now; it's a faith thing. I think people who have metal in their bodies and need healing can come into a faith for that condition.

**Bill:** I agree completely. I think that's what happened with the leg lengthening thing from the charismatic movement. But to me, the sad part is to think that someone who has an anointing for one thing just stays there instead of using that as an experiment to springboard into something else. Because we've had an experience where it was the testimony of clubfeet being healed that brought a miracle of healing to a completely different injury. The clubfeet were close enough—in the foot. Do you know what I mean? If you're getting breakthrough with leg lengthening, then why not look for other injuries to the leg—for example, bones that didn't heal in the leg—and go for that? Or no cartilage in the knee—start going for that. Why? Because it's in a realm where you're getting breakthrough.

That's why I think we owe it to the Lord, to ourselves and to the people we serve to use our breakthrough as momentum to get breakthrough in more areas. I'll look for a related condition; I'll look for something that's similar. We've had bizarre cases of healing by approaching things that way.

A gal in Australia had no cartilage in her knees, and her husband had to retire to take care of her. The pain she suffered because of having her bone-on-bone condition was so great that doctors refer to it as "suicidal measure pain." The husband spent $25,000 putting a lift in his home so he could get his wife up to the second floor so she could still stay in their bedroom. She came to the meeting and got so dramatically healed that she was sprinting around the room. She was a very timid Asian lady, but she grabbed the mic and started yelling. The entire church knew her, and they were stunned at the miracle.

When I see that happening, I start thinking, *Wait a minute, some people have fused spines with discs missing. The conditions aren't related, yet they are.* . . . Does that make sense? We can use breakthrough in one area to push into another realm of breakthrough. That's how I think we develop this stuff.

**Randy:** I'm just thinking of the parallel that I've seen of that. I had never seen a stroke victim healed, but after I heard about Heidi Baker and the dead being raised, that's when we had three stroke victims healed in 24 hours. The concept was, *Okay, if God is healing the dead, He has to rebuild their cells. That's also what's needed in strokes and Parkinson's and MS. . . .* So it gives you faith to really begin to press into new and related areas with more expectation.

# 4

# Electric Experiences and Breakthrough Events

**Randy:** Bill, let's switch to the next question, though it's very much related to what we've already talked about. We may have already covered it, but were there any breakthrough events in your life that caused you to see more? I'm curious about the relationship between breakthrough and the electrifying story you tell. . . .

**Bill:** The all-night experience!

**Randy:** Yes, the three o'clock in the morning story. Did you see any connection between that event and a breakthrough in healing, or an increase or breakthrough of power in something else? I know the one experience I had late at night was my most powerful, but other than a deliverance thing, I couldn't really point to any more power in any area for several years. But I know experiences like that are key; I know that electric event was the most powerful thing you ever had happen. And then other times, there was less intensity, but it was significant. Your late-night experience almost killed you, it was so powerful. But then immediate fruit came out of that one. It's kind of odd; you can't make a formula out of it.

**Bill:** True, there's not always a correlation. I already mentioned that I was in Weaverville and had gone to Toronto in February 1995, then we started to get a breakthrough in April or May. And then another one in August. Then a friend of ours, Dick Joyce, came, and it blew up. That's when I had the 3:00 A.M. encounter—October of 1995.

**Randy:** How bizarre! I was actually in that same Toronto meeting in February 1995 that you attended! And I was just thinking, the experience I had where I thought I was going to die wasn't that same year, but it also happened in October. There really are some amazing parallels between us. I love your story, though. Tell us what happened.

**Bill:** Our church had been involved in the renewal, and we were starting to experience new things. We had a weekly Friday night prayer meeting where a lot of stuff was happening and we learned a lot about how the Holy Spirit moves, so we kind of turned that into a prayer/renewal meeting. And we brought Dick in. He had been with us in Toronto in February, and he had already been ministering in power and seeing stuff happen. For years, people would fall when he prayed for them.

Toronto had impacted me internally, although I didn't walk out with the kind of breakthrough anointing I now realize you can get in those kinds of gatherings. But we started getting a measure of breakthrough, and in October we had these meetings with Dick that were electric. During that time, I prophesied to a friend who was struggling that God was going to touch him, maybe at 3:00 in the morning. I went home late—you know all these meetings run late, so you get to bed in the wee hours. At 3:00 A.M. exactly, the electricity of God hit me. I was at a dead sleep; I was exhausted. Dead sleep. And I was instantly as awake as I could be, and there wasn't but a millisecond in between those two realities. I was completely awake. I knew it. I could move my head and I knew enough to look at the clock—3:00 A.M. And God reminded me of my prophecy to my friend. As I was lying in bed, I said out loud, "You set me up, Lord." Because my arms were shooting up, my legs were shooting up, and I had no control of my body. This went on for several minutes. I kept thinking, *It's going to lift*. It didn't lift. Finally, I pulled my arms next to my side, and my legs got more violent. It was as though power was flowing through me at such a high level that if I tried to control one thing, another thing got worse. And so I realized, *It's God. I don't know what He's doing!*

It wasn't comfortable at all. It wasn't pleasant. Honestly, it was somewhat miserable in the way it felt. It was aggravating in one sense. But at the same time, I had such an awareness of God's presence that there wasn't even the slightest temptation to want it to go away, because I knew this was my moment. This power was going through me. I laid there wondering, *What's going on?*

Beni didn't wake up. We were in a water bed, and I thought it was a miracle all by itself that she wasn't tidal waved out of the bed! As this was going on, God reminded me that I had been praying nonstop day and night for more. I would wake up praying. Or rather, I wouldn't wake up *to pray*—I would wake up because I *was praying* in my sleep. And I'd be praying for more: "God, You've got to give me more. I've got to have more. I will pay any price. I've got to have more."

*You've been praying for more at any price*, God said, and then scenes started going through my mind. I saw myself trying to teach in front of the church in Weaverville; I love to teach the Word. And I saw people reacting to my physical manifestation. They were going to think I was crazy! Nobody in their right minds would think this was God, because it wasn't stopping.

Then I saw myself in front of my favorite restaurant in town, reacting physically like this. And I realized, *I'm going to be a laughingstock not only to the church, but to the entire city. I'm going to look as if I need to be locked up.*

I remembered Jacob wrestling with the angel and how he walked with a limp the rest of his life. I remembered how Mary was accused of being "the mother of an illegitimate child." That was her label the rest of her life. And after all those thoughts had gone through my mind, I realized what God was after. He wanted to know if He could have my dignity.

There wasn't a moment's hesitation in me. I said, "You can have it. Just give me more." That's what I told Him. "You can have it, if I get You in the exchange."

The other crazy thought going on in my mind was, *I don't know how I will ever get out of bed.* It's hard to explain moments like that; it doesn't make any sense to just talk about them. But that's what was going on in my mind: *If this keeps on, I don't know if I'll ever get out of bed because it feels as if it's blowing circuits where I'm going to lose the physical capacity to function normally as a husband, as a father, as a pastor.*

I saw these scenes and I realized I might never get out of bed again, and I said to the Lord, "All right—if I get You in the exchange, Your presence, if that's what I get. You take away my capacity to function, but give me more of You. I'll do it." And then all night long, I just lay there praying, "Just increase it, just go deeper. Don't stop, just go deeper, increase it."

It lasted until 6:38. At that time, I got out of bed. Almost any day that I see 6:38 on a clock, I give thanks now. It's a trigger for me to know that God deposited something. I can't trace back what; all I know is that there has been continuous breakthrough since that week and since that night—continuous breakthrough. I got out of bed and went about the day as if I'd had eight hours of sleep, though I slept hardly at all. I'd been wide awake. And it started again the moment I got in bed the next night, and then on a third night. It actually happened for three nights.

**Randy:** How long did it last the second and third nights?

**Bill:** I don't even know because I just lay there praying, "Increase it!" The third night it hit Beni, too. So we both were laying there just absolutely being electrocuted. And it went on for quite a while. Not all night; we did get some sleep. But it lasted a significant amount of time. When morning came, I was glad I was able to get up and function, the same as I had been at 6:38 the first morning.

It was as if God were Roto-Rootering us, Randy. He was doing something to clean us out and get us ready for a Holy Spirit lifestyle that I quite frankly only knew through worship. I knew the presence in worship, but I didn't know it in an anointing and I didn't know it in ministry. I had inspired thought in my teachings—I knew that world. But I didn't know the presence in any kind of power ministry. So that connected me.

**Randy:** Were there any other breakthrough events where you can look back and say, "You know, these two, three, four things . . . after each one, there was breakthrough and increase"?

**Bill:** One was the first time I went with you to Brazil and Argentina. You remember the trip where we didn't get any sleep for nineteen days? We sat up on a bus for two hours at a time, getting sleep between cities.

**Randy:** That was a crazy trip. Earlier I was wondering if you remembered our trip to Argentina where we had Ben Scofield along. He was nineteen or twenty, and he was my first intern, the first one God told me to take along. I put $60,000 in him in two years, paying his way to travel with me. He's the only one God said to do that for. All the other interns had to pay their own way. That's not true now, of course, because now my interns travel free. But there was a season where interns had to pay to be interns. But anyway, Ben was the first, and you and Ben were praying for this person who had a growth on the top of his foot, an extra bone or something. It was about the size of your finger.

**Bill:** I'll never forget that as long as I live. The cool thing was that in the service, you had called out a word of knowledge and said, "There's somebody who has a problem over the top of each of your feet."

You were very specific. And this maybe fourteen-year-old kid came up because of that word. He took his shoe and sock off so we could see one foot, and I put my thumb on the top. Ben took hold of his other foot. I put my thumb on the extra bone and commanded it to dissolve and didn't do anything else. We just sat there for another minute, maybe two minutes. All of a sudden it was as if a balloon were deflating. And I started feeling around and said, "Would you check that out!"

And the kid said, "It's gone!"

So I said, "Well, let's pray for the other one!" And he took the other sock and shoe off, and that one was already gone. Oh my goodness, it was stunning to have something disappear like that! The extra bone had just dissolved under my fingers.

I'll never forget it, or the way you had the word of knowledge about the tops of both his feet.

**Randy:** I had forgotten that part, but I do remember both your response and Ben's afterward—I remember the look on your faces.

**Bill:** It was a weird deformity. You know how your knuckles have a certain kind of skin to them, where the other part of your hands or feet doesn't? He had that kind of skin over that extra bone because for fourteen years of his life, his shoes had rubbed over the top of it. It was almost like an elbow-type skin that formed over those bones. And when we prayed, they were gone. There was nothing there. It was fascinating, so fascinating.

**Randy:** I love the fascinating part where you wonder, *How did that happen?*

**Bill:** Right. You wonder, *Did I see what I just think I saw?* That trip had great impact on me. All the trips—I've done so many, and they all have impacted me. But that was the first one. You and I were actually just getting acquainted in many ways on that trip. You'd been to Redding, but you invited me to Brazil, so I went. I'll never be the same.

**Randy:** Can you think of any other events that had significant impact on you?

**Bill:** I've had a few encounters in the last year that were some of the most extreme of my life. I don't know how they'll play out. I was with Oral Roberts in his home about six weeks before he died. About thirty of us were there. They ended up placing me right next to him, so I sat and just listened and tried to glean

61

as much as I could. Then there came a time when he wanted to pray for us, so I knelt in front of him. He said to me, "What do you want?"

I said, "I want your anointing. I want your breakthrough."

He laid his hands on me, and he went "Whoa!" and jerked his arm. He said, "I won't ask you if you felt that one—it about blew my arm off."

It rang my bell, I tell you! It whacked me! And it didn't happen the rest of the time he was praying. It wasn't a normal thing, from what I understand. His arm absolutely shot out and just whacked me. And honestly, I've had three things happen to me in the last thirteen months that I've been praying about on this fast I'm on. Something happened in those events that will take a while to unravel. Oral Roberts praying over me was the first one.

And then last January, Ché Ahn and I were in Korea. (Ché Ahn is the apostolic leader of HROCK Church in Pasadena and of a network of churches called Harvest International Ministry.) We got to meet with Dr. David Yonggi Cho in a private meeting—private meaning with cameras and his security—but still a private meeting. And he laid hands on us. It was fascinating. But before Ché could ask him to pray for us, we were just talking with him, and he said, "You know, Dr. Roberts was the greatest inspiration of my life."

We didn't bring up Oral Roberts, and I had just met him. I was just with him maybe three months earlier. And Dr. Cho started talking about Dr. Oral Roberts and the inspiration he was, the help and counsel he was, and what a father he was. . . . I sat there thinking, *Man, this is a setup. This is a setup!* I was still reeling from my encounter with Oral Roberts.

Ché said to Dr. Cho, "We'd love for you to pray for us."

Dr. Cho said, "Oh, I need for you to pray for me." But we knelt in front of him, Ché first and then me. I had specific things

I was praying in my heart, and Dr. Cho prayed exactly those things—line upon line—everything that was in my heart.

Then three weeks ago, I was at an international healing conference in Minneapolis. You and I did that one together a few years ago. This time, Claudio Freidzon was there. I've been with him before. I've been with Carlos Annacondia and you together a couple of times. I've been with Claudio before, and it was wonderful, glorious—I just love the guy. But something happened this time. We were in a lunch meeting together. I spoke first, and it really went well. The Lord was really moving. It was one of those moments where He was moving in revelation. It was a twenty-minute deal, but it was like an hour and a half's worth of stuff. It was just one of those unusual moments. And Claudio followed me up there and was impacted, which was encouraging to me. And then he went into ministry time. He came and laid hands on me, and I have never had this happen, but my feet shot up in the air. I got shot, like with a gun. I've never had my feet go like that. I've crumpled before, and I've had times where you and Rodney Howard-Browne have prayed for me and it was really something, but this time my feet shot up in the air and I fell. I don't remember hitting the ground. There was no thud; there was nothing. As far as I could tell you, I never hit the ground. I've heard of that happening, but I had never experienced anything like it. I hit the ground soft as a pillow, just hit the ground but don't remember anything. It wasn't jarring or painful, nothing like that. He proceeded to pray over me many more times that day, and again in the night meeting.

I'll tell you what, I don't know what happened, but when I went home, stuff started happening at church. It was like coming home from Anaheim the first time, where we'd seen people falling under that power like we'd never seen happen before. It was that kind of a release in the church. I didn't even talk about it, I just told the people, "I had a great encounter with Claudio Freidzon this week." I kept it simple; I didn't elaborate on anything. But stuff started happening that was fresh for us.

I don't know how, but I think these encounters will play out even more over time.

**Randy:** You briefly mentioned this fast you're doing. Is this the first time for the kind you're on right now? Or is this a second or third time? And is there a certain reason? How did you get called into it?

**Bill:** The fast? This is the first 40-day fast for me. I've done 30 days, 21 days and 14 days before, but I've never done 40. There are two main reasons. The timing of this fast is connected to the elections and the fact that there has been this call to fast and pray. Generally with something like this, we'll fast for a few days, or maybe we'll go on a Daniel fast or skip meals every other day. We'll do something different. But this time, I just felt this grace to do 40 days. I looked at my schedule, and it was bizarre. I've had up to four conferences back to back without a break, which is weird to do while you're fasting. But I felt a grace for it. And I've had a crazy strength, just crazy strength to do what I'm doing on this schedule while fasting. There was just a grace for it, for the country.

But also, I've got to have greater breakthrough. There're a lot of promises, a lot of things I've seen that the Lord wants to do. There are realms in God that are available that I haven't touched. And I'm just so hungry; there's this deep desire in me for more. You just get hungrier for that than you do for food—and that's called a fast.

Back in 1987—let alone 1977—I never would have thought that what we're experiencing right now was possible. But now it's normal, and that has ruined me. Now this will never do because we still have history behind us where those who went before us excelled, where they had realms of breakthrough that we've not touched yet. And until we recover all that has been lost, we can't truly explore what God wants to do. That's part of what we're focusing on with our House of Generals—our library and all this material we're collecting that honors some of these generals from the past, these revivalists we can learn so much from. I believe that the Lord is going to give us access to their anointing.

# 5

# SEEING AND HEARING
# GOD MOVE

**Randy:** Before it gets too late and we start dropping—I think it's now 1:00 in the morning—I want to ask you, Bill, if there's anything else you want to say about how your ability developed to see and hear what the Lord is doing in regard to healing?

**Bill:** I can't trace it back to one encounter or a single prophecy or anything like that, Randy. But what I can trace it back to are all the renewal meetings and the explosive releases of power and anointing. You start developing an eye for what the Lord is doing. I can't explain it; I would walk through a zone and realize, *Man, there's something here. I'm going to assume it's an angelic presence.* I could feel it, and I could see with my senses when there were certain things happening. So I'd take somebody who was struggling and put them in that area.

You just get into these times where, if you don't stop and analyze it, you start flowing with it. I analyze it later—I just start cooperating with it in the moment. That starts training your senses to pick up on the move of God.

I would start sensing things on a Sunday morning before the service. I'd go down to the church and pray early, and I'd start picking up on what was going to happen in certain parts of the room. A yielded imagination becomes a sanctified imagination, and a sanctified imagination is positioned for visions and dreams. Its position is to pick things up. So I'd walk around the room on Sunday morning and find myself daydreaming about certain things taking place in a certain part of the room. I soon realized that I needed to write things down because something was about to happen. That's one of the ways God would prepare me for what was about to happen.

In these electric, explosive times of God's power and anointing, you start getting trained to recognize what He's doing. But where that started for me, way back in the early '70s, was in worship. It was first learning to recognize the presence, and then God would start coming explosively, which I wasn't used to. I was used to the calm presence in the charismatic renewal, you know. Kum-ba-yah, almost. It was glorious and wonderful, but He started coming explosively and I had to learn to recognize what was about to happen. It's easy to recognize somebody flying across the room when it happens, but it's something else to learn from that so you can see what's about to happen on this side of the room. Then you're a participant. You're seeing what He's wanting to have happen through co-labor. That's a huge deal for me, learning to recognize that.

It's the overall scope of things that helped me develop that. By being alongside people, for example, working with you when you're in these crusades and you're preaching, it would develop. I'd be off to the side, and I could see and feel what was happening. The training schools, too, these healing schools, develop that.

I learn so much by watching how you navigate with what the Holy Spirit is doing. I'm always asking God, "Show me what's about to happen, because I want to learn how Randy picks it up."

It's not always a conscious thing, picking up on what God is doing. Sometimes it's just that a conviction falls on me. I don't know of a better way to describe it. I'll look, and I'll have a conviction about something. And I'll know, *Okay, I don't have time to stop and analyze this, I just need to act because something's about to happen here.* It may be that in a certain realm, healings are about to happen. I'll have a conviction, for example, that *God is about to do something right now about healing head trauma,* or whatever. But there will be that conviction.

It's learning to recognize the presence. I think the Lord wants us to learn to recognize His presence by Himself. (I make this distinction because it becomes easy to recognize God's presence by what He does. I want to recognize His presence *before* He does anything. In other words, I'm trying to learn to recognize Him, by Himself.) But sometimes He will only manifest upon another person. So if I can't shift my focus to the anointing that rests on you, or on Rodney, or on whomever, then sometimes I'm going to miss some of the lessons He has for me. Part of the process for me has been learning to recognize the Spirit of God on another person and watching how they navigate in the anointing. That's huge for me.

**Randy:** That has also been important for me when we've done things together, because in the last two years I've seen such a phenomenal leap in you. And I've thought, *Man, I've not seen Bill do this before.* Like when you began to declare that something is done. You'll tell someone, "Check it out; it's done." And I'll sit there with my jaw dropping, thinking, *How does he know that?*

Watching you, I've been able to see it, and I've been wanting to step out in it. And you encourage me, saying, "You're getting more than you're saying. You need to declare it."

It's been good, our mutual encouragement. All the things you've talked about in this interview help me so much, and they'll help others develop, too.

# 6

# KEEPING THE TESTIMONY

**Randy:** I'd like to conclude this time with you, Bill, by asking you to share with us the four or five stories of the greatest healings you've seen.

**Bill:** I especially like telling stories of healings that took place in the United States, Randy, because they've been so rare historically. But those kinds of testimonies are finally back! First, though, I want to tell you about a healing that happened in Brazil that was pretty fun, pretty significant. I prayed for a woman who had a tumor probably the size of a melon. Some of the team had been praying for her for quite a while. I went over and joined them, kind of in agreement, and put my hand on the tumor. It was on her abdomen, and it just vanished. It's one thing to have an extra little bone vanish on a boy's foot; we talked about that healing earlier. That was impressive. But when a tumor the size of a melon just disappears, that's extremely noteworthy, extremely impressive.

The healings I like the most, and we have a series of them, involve missing muscle. It all started so interestingly. One person got healed, gave a testimony, and an anointing came for others who had the same problem. Three or four people in that room had the same problem—that's weird. How many people in a city are missing the same part of the same muscle? Then miracles with missing muscle tissue continued for months and months, actually years. It's fascinating to watch how God creatively restores missing muscle and other things. I'm just wild about it.

Here's a United States story, Randy. We had a missionary from Sudan come to our church. The Lord had told her (in a dream), *If you get to Redding, I'll heal you.*

This missionary had MS, she had West Nile virus and she had ME (myalgic encephalomyelitis) and fibromyalgia. They wouldn't let her out of Sudan because of those problems, so she had to sneak out of the country. She had this dream, so she flew all the way to Redding. By the time she arrived, the West Nile virus was already gone. I remember praying over her. MS has been particularly frustrating for us because we've lost some courageous warriors, one in particular, through that horrible disease. We've spent a lot of time contending in secret, "God, give us breakthrough with MS."

This missionary came, and within fifteen minutes she was completely set free of MS! Where it would have been difficult for her to walk from here to there (about fifteen feet), she could now sprint around the room. She was absolutely, absolutely healed. That's a big one for us, because we've waged such a battle with that particular disease.

We've also had other fascinating things happen in recent months. We had a guy come who was a rowdy, cantankerous old biker. Never been to church in his life, but his son had gotten saved. This old biker was dying of cancer, so his son said,

"Dad, I think you need to come up to Redding, and they'll pray for your cancer."

I think the guy lived in Fresno or somewhere, and he growled at his son that he didn't want anything to do with that kind of stuff. But he was getting worse, so he finally thought, *All right, I'll go.*

He came into our healing rooms on a Saturday morning, and three people came over to pray for him. He told them, "You can pray for me, but don't touch me. I don't want any of that hocus-pocus stuff."

He stood there and watched those three people, and finally he relaxed enough to close his eyes. Well, a twelve-year-old kid on another healing team saw this old biker and walked over and put his hand on his chest. The kid didn't know that the guy had said, "Don't touch me."

As soon as the twelve-year-old put his hands on the guy's chest, the guy went flying back, and he was out for an extended period of time. He got up completely healed. He went back to the VA hospital, and the doctors confirmed that he had no cancer. They interviewed him and interviewed him, demanding, "Now tell us *again* what happened." He finally had a brochure made with a map of how to get from Fresno to Redding and how to get to Bethel Church. He would give it to the doctors when they would ask him about his healing. And he printed out his testimony.

This guy got dramatically saved and started bringing people every other week—sick people—in his car. He literally picked up this woman who'd been bedridden for a long time, put her in his car and said, "You're coming with me." He drove her to Redding, and she got dramatically healed.

When they were driving back to Fresno, the woman told him, "Pull over."

"All right," he said, pulling over. "Why?"

The woman answered, "I haven't driven in five years—I'm driving!" So she got in the driver's seat, and they continued on their way.

Dramatic things like that have started happening. We have over 400 people sometimes on a Saturday. That's a conference! A small Saturday would be 150 to 200 people. So we have a worship team in the healing rooms, and also painters who are painting. One day, one of our painters painted the word *hope*. And this woman who had come, who had Stage IV brain cancer, walked over to that painting. Staring at the word *hope*, she started crying. People rallied around her to find out if she was okay. She turned to them and said, "You don't understand—my tunnel vision just left. And the pressure on my brain is gone!" Fluid also started draining from her ear. She went back to the doctor and it was confirmed—she had no more cancer.

One Sunday night we had a guy dancing up and down in the middle of the room, holding his pants up because the four large tumors that had held his pants up before were gone. He had been given a month to live. He was standing in the middle of the sanctuary, oblivious to everything else that was going on, holding his pants up and saying, "Oh, my gosh! Oh, my gosh! Oh, my gosh!" His pants would have fallen down around his ankles if he hadn't been holding them up after the tumors disappeared.

**Randy:** Did that one happen sovereignly, like during worship or a testimony? Or were people praying for him?

**Bill:** That one was sovereign. I don't remember if it was during worship or what, but nobody prayed for him.

We also had esophagus cancer healed sovereignly. The gal who had it turned to her husband in the service because heat just came out of her hands and she said, "I've just been healed."

The heat didn't touch her throat; it touched her hands. She translated that as the anointing for healing. It was a faith thing on her part.

Afterward, they went to the doctor so she could be reexamined. The doctor, who previously had told her that this kind of cancer never goes away, examined her and said, "Not only do you not have cancer—you have a brand-new esophagus!"

**Randy:** I love the creative miracles!

**Bill:** On one of my trips to New Zealand, we had a guy who was on a kidney transplant list and the Lord gave him his own new kidney, which was quite amazing.

But you know, I consider some of the simplest miracles to be the greatest ones. I'm fascinated by situations where there's no cartilage, for example, and then miraculously there's cartilage.

Honestly, I'm fascinated by a feather floating down. Out of nothing, something appeared. If God is doing it, I just want to delight in it and celebrate it. I've honestly been thinking about a feather appearing and floating down, realizing it had to be created out of nothing. If God can do that, then He can certainly creatively put a part back in the body. He can certainly restore the brain cells damaged by Parkinson's disease or whatever. To me, it's all connected, but those are some of the greatest miracles.

(This issue of feathers appearing has become quite a controversy. Honestly, if I were going to ask for God to do something supernatural, I wouldn't ask for feathers. It seems to be more of an item that attracts criticism and skepticism than anything. But that doesn't seem to bother the Lord. It comes with the territory of moving with God. He likes to see if we'll be embarrassed by what He does. Will we fear man or fear God? It really comes down to that. As for the phenomenon, it's really simple. Feathers appear out of nowhere. I first thought we had birds nesting in our air-conditioning ducts at the church. Then feathers fell in other buildings at the church, at home and in restaurants. It's a sign that makes you wonder. It doesn't need to have more purpose than that for me. I don't need to understand or get some profound message from it. I simply celebrate it as an act of God. Acts of God are not to be valued by the outcome. They are valued because they are from God.)

Our first deaf person was quite fascinating, too. She had never heard a sound in her life; she was 100 percent deaf. I remember her being healed at a Sunday night meeting during a renewal. People were getting whacked all over the room. Someone prayed for her, and she started pointing to the ceiling, where the speakers were. Somebody said, "We just had a deaf woman healed," so I ran over to talk to her.

"How are you hearing? How did it happen?" I asked her. It took me a minute to remember that since she had never spoken, she didn't know any words. I suddenly realized in that moment that she didn't understand a word I was saying. *Oh, my goodness,* I thought, *she's never heard anything like words in her life.* Over the next several days, her relatives started training her in speaking. It was fascinating.

We had a gal at a renewal meeting fall and break her foot while she was dancing around at the back of the room. As an emergency room nurse, she knew when bones were broken. Hers wasn't sticking through the skin, but it was pushing at the edge of the skin. She came up to one of the people in the room and said, "Do you believe God will heal this?"

He replied, "I'll pray for you."

She said, "You're not the one." She went to someone else, one of our speakers, and said, "Do you believe God will heal this? I just broke my foot."

He replied the same as the first guy, "I'll pray for you."

She said, "You're not the one." She went to Cal Pierce (this was before he moved up to Spokane) and said, "Do you believe God will heal this? I just broke my foot."

Cal replied, "Yeah, I do."

He prayed, and the bone went right back into place. She was completely healed; she was able to dance and do everything moments later. We've had tons of broken bones healed.

**Randy:** Did you know that kind of miracle happened tonight? A woman came in just after she stepped into a hole. Her broken foot was all bandaged up. It was a recent break, and she was in a lot of pain. She couldn't put any weight on it. I had dinner with this couple, in fact, right before the service. Her husband was one of the people who came up for ordination and licensing. She came in on crutches.

**Bill:** Actually, they put her in a wheelchair after she had dinner with you.

**Randy:** Right. During worship, no one prayed for her. After worship we invited people up for ordination and licensing, and she came up with her husband and motioned to me and said, "I've been healed in worship!" It happened tonight.

**Bill:** I know this interview has gone long, but let me tell you about one thing I've noticed. I've experimented with it sporadically, and we've tested and measured it. If I say at the beginning of a meeting, "It's normal for tumors to disappear in the presence of the Lord," 80 or 90 percent of the time, tumors will disappear in that meeting. If I don't say it and we just pray for tumors, it's not as likely to happen.

**Randy:** I would concur with some of that principle. It's not a principle that I think works for anyone and everyone—for example, it's not for New Agers who believe they can create their own reality with their words. But in the context you're talking about, Bill, I totally agree. Declarations based on faith in God and in His faithfulness can make a huge difference, just as you described.

Do you have an expectation about how many people will be healed, percentage-wise, in a meeting, both in other countries and in the United States? Do you ever announce, "I know God is going to heal, and I expect it to be at least this many . . ."?

**Bill:** I think I've done that a couple of times. I've watched it happen with you. It happened last night or the night before. It was amazing. You called out the number, and it was exactly that number. I haven't pushed into that one.

**Randy:** I got excited about that one. It was twenty and then six. That was so fun for me because it was like, *Wow, I heard from heaven. I really did.*

It wasn't a word of knowledge, though, and it wasn't even a gift of faith. But it is a kind of faith. Do you know what I mean? For me to have a gift of faith has been quite rare, the kind where I know a certain thing is going to happen. I really believe if you have the gift of faith like that, whatever you say happens. If it doesn't, it really wasn't the gift of faith. The gift of faith has creative miracle power.

With the numbers, wherever I've been, I've always kept watching. I've always kept counting and keeping track of the number of people getting healed. When we went to your church, it was a big breakthrough in numbers for me. Up to that point at churches your size, where there were about a thousand at a time in a meeting, we'd typically have about thirty get saved or rededicated, thirty go through deliverance and thirty get healed. Thirty out of a thousand is 3 percent. That's what we were hitting. And I'll never forget the night the breakthrough happened. I counted twenty-five healings that came through a word of knowledge. Then if you remember, I had an impression.

**Bill:** I do remember.

**Randy:** The impression was as though the Lord said, "I want you to be like Abraham, but I want you to go the other direction according to the measure of your faith."

So I told the crowd, "This is what I felt that God just said. . . ." And I asked them, "Do you think He's tired?"

"No!"

"Do you think He's run out of power?"

"No!"

"I'm going to ask Him for 50 healings."

We prayed and we counted, and I think there were 45 or 50, somewhere in there. So we did it again, and this time asked Him for 75. And on the third time, there were exactly 75. That was three times the normal number for this size crowd. The thing I learned that night about asking for more is that what you ask for builds faith, so I asked for 100. We counted, and there were over 100! Maybe 125 or 134 or something.

**Bill:** I think there were 129.

**Randy:** Afterward, somebody came up to me and said, "Why did you take all that time? Why didn't you just ask God to heal 100 people to start with?"

That person didn't get the principle at all. God said to ask "according to the measure of your faith." According to my measure of faith, I couldn't go from 25 to 100 people. I knew my expectation wasn't there at the start. But I learned a huge lesson in that meeting, and I have followed it in a lot of meetings since. We'll get to a certain point, and I'll think, *That's not enough glory for God. That's not strong enough.* And I'll ask Him for more, and the measure of my faith will increase.

After that, I really started to pay attention to the numbers. I figured that in the United States back at that time, out of the total number of people present, we'd see about 10 percent minimum healed. (This took place prior to the last few years, during which we've seen a much bigger breakthrough.) So we were in Brazil one time, and it hit me. I made what looked like a faith statement, but it really wasn't. You were with me. They had about eight thousand people in a covered arena, and it seemed huge to me. It was the biggest thing I'd seen up to that time.

I got up, and right off the bat I made a declaration. I can't say it was a faith declaration, not like the gift of faith, but it was spoken in faith. And after that night, I would start making this kind of declaration almost everywhere I went. I knew 10 percent of the people there would get healed, and the way I knew was that I had always been counting the numbers, as I said. And there had always been at least 10 percent; that's the minimum. So I got up and declared, "Before we leave tonight, there will be at least eight hundred people who get healed."

The crowd went crazy! And I was thinking, *They don't know that would be the minimum. There're eight thousand here, and eight hundred is just 10 percent. That's simply the minimum number we've been seeing.*

To me, that kind of declaration builds faith, and it's not presumptuous. Alan Hawkins, a friend and an experienced pastor who acts as one of my pastoral advisors, once told me he used to think I was presumptuous, and I explained it to him this way: "Alan, it wasn't presumption at all. It was that I had faith in God's faithfulness because I'd watched Him heal 10 percent so many times."

I actually had a real expectation for a minimum of 10 percent healings, wherever we were. I would have been shocked if it wasn't at least that much anywhere. I think it's something that is a principle. I think that what we see, we actually come into faith for after we've seen it enough. And it's not presumption, not at all. It's just a faith that "I know God is going to do this!"

**Bill:** The way I describe that kind of thing is that I feel as though I have a realm in God; I have ownership of something. When I don't know what to do in a meeting, I can start with what I *know* God has done in the past. That's what you're talking about, that kind of proclamation. In your case, it's about declaring how many people will be healed in a meeting. In my case, maybe it's declaring, "Tumors will disappear in the presence of the Lord." But I use that same thing. It's the same concept. Using our momentum in God—what we have going in God—we can make a declaration or call out a condition.

I might announce, for example, "The Lord is going to heal accident victims right now." I don't need a word of knowledge for that; I've got no inspiration, in a sense. It's just that this is my history with God. This is my history, and we've got momentum going in that area of healing.

**Randy:** The one thing I have that with is healings where people have metal in their bodies. That's it.

**Bill:** That's a big one. That's so bizarre—the most bizarre thing that you have happening is the easiest one for you to call out.

**Randy:** And I can't explain it, but I get so excited about it. I know I haven't had anything to do with this—other than declare that

God is going to heal people with metal. Out of the last thirteen months and all the meetings we've had, there are only three times that somebody did not get healed of a problem with metal. The first time it didn't happen, it freaked me out because I really was expecting it to happen. Then there was a little church in Paris where only one or two people had any metal in them. Same thing at one other place where there were only two or three people who had metal. That was just recently, but other than those three instances, God has healed metal every time. I know it's not my faith—I don't have faith in my faith. But I've seen God be so faithful. I have a faith that has been created out of His faithfulness in this area. I wouldn't dare do this in any other area at this point. It wouldn't be true or integrous with what I really know.

**Bill:** Right, because you and I don't want to make statements just to hype. That's the last thing in the world we want to do. But you start picking up stuff in certain areas, and you can feel God's heart in things. So that's where I learned to make a declaration, not just on a whim, but out of a conviction that this is normal in the Kingdom, so you just declare it. And it starts happening.

**Randy:** It's 1:30 A.M., and our one-hour interview has turned into two. I'm delighted with it, and I thank you for taking the time. I had so much fun interviewing you, and I learned so much from you. It's just like iron sharpening iron. I believe this particular interview will be very helpful to those growing in this ministry of healing. It will give clues and insights to people as they hunger to see more happen. And I know that we'll do this again. We'll just keep taking notes and be ready to exchange them with each other. Eventually I want to have many of these kinds of interviews available to students at Global Awakening's school, maybe as part of a Christian Healing Certification Program. Right now, some of our courses are lecture and clinic, and some are all lecture. The course we'd put together out of what we're doing here would be all interview, and it will be a fantastic help and encouragement to people.

**Bill:** That's excellent. I look forward to doing more of these. I've enjoyed it.

**Randy:** I want to say something to all the people watching these DVDs or reading this book about our interviews. This is a time of golden opportunity for you to learn. Between the two of us, Bill and I have almost 80 years of ministry experience. Bill, how long have you been in ministry?

**Bill:** I've been at it for 37 years now.

**Randy:** And I've been at it for 40, so that's 77 combined years of ministry between us. We're not that old—we just started young!

Speaking of interviews, I had the opportunity to interview my dad like this about his whole life. The interview was an hour or two, and it's precious. I was interviewing him on GarageBand (a software program for recording) and found out stuff I never knew about him. When my son Josh, who is 29, saw it, he came up to me and said, "Dad, I want to do that with you."

I said, "Son, my dad is 79 years old. I'm only 59! We need to wait awhile."

Josh said, "No, I want to do it now, while you can still remember. And then I'll do it again when you're older, before you forget stuff."

**Bill:** That's hilarious!

**Randy:** So, for those who are watching or reading these interviews, Bill and I got stuff down while we're still able to remember it. I know there are things a person doesn't forget, but there are details you do forget.

Bill, do you keep a journal of some of the more dramatic insights and healings in your ministry?

**Bill:** I used to do that, and I'm toying with starting again. I have to create systems to be consistent about something like that.

**Randy:** I know I can't journal, but I've asked Chad Cromer to do it in the past. (He was my personal assistant for over a year and did an awesome job—it took two guys to replace him!) Chad would write down the stories of just the people who were on the stage and gave the testimony. We have all the stories of the healings that we have on camera within the last twelve months. One day I sat down and started reading the record because I can't remember all this stuff. I read like twenty pages of it, and it sure makes you stop and wonder at the amazing things God is doing. My faith was so high after that! Someday I want to do a little book, not spanning a whole lifetime, but just recording one year of what God has done. "Here's what we caught in a year. . . ." It would build faith!

**Bill:** Mary Berck, my personal assistant, records the healing stories for me. She writes them down, and it's so helpful. It's really encouraging, as you said, to go back through them.

**Randy:** Thanks again, Bill, for taking the time to do this. It was great.

**Bill:** Thanks, Randy. I liked it, and I learned from it.

**Randy:** I did, too.

# PART 2

# BILL JOHNSON
# INTERVIEWS
# RANDY CLARK

# 7

# A HUNGER FOR HEALING

**Bill:** I have the great privilege today of interviewing Randy Clark, who is probably the most influential person in my life in the area of miracles, signs and wonders. His whole lifestyle exemplifies living a Spirit-filled life, where God shows up and does extraordinary things. I wish that as a younger man, I could have asked more questions of people like Randy who impacted my life spiritually and made a mark on history. In this particular event, we have the privilege of doing just that. I'll be asking Randy some important questions about his spiritual journey past and present, and I'm looking forward to hearing what he has to say and learning from his answers.

To start off, Randy, what events and experiences in your life really led you specifically into a healing ministry? How did your whole anointing for miracle breakthroughs start?

**Randy:** I think, Bill, the initial thing that caught my interest in healing was my maternal grandmother's experience of it. She had a large goiter in her throat back before doctors discovered how to treat them with iodine. As a new Christian living in a little four-room, cement block house, she heard the audible voice of God tell her, "Go into the other bedroom and pray, and I'll heal you." She didn't ask, "Why not right here?" With childlike faith, she simply went into the other bedroom and started praying. She told me she felt as if a hot hand went down her throat, and the goiter instantly vanished. I was between four and five years old when she told me that story, and I never forgot it. It created a hunger in me for healing.

At the same age, I would sit on my great-grandmother's lap and watch Oral Roberts on a black-and-white TV. Even today I can remember sitting there watching the whole show, and I would be fixated on the healing lines.

Then when I was six, my mother had an experience with the reality of God and the supernatural. She was taken out of her body and went to heaven. For days afterward—in fact, for the next forty years—she couldn't tell about it without crying. Dad was backslidden at the time it happened, giving her a hard time, and she had three little kids to take care of while he was off working a lot of hours. Jesus came up to Mom, and without talking, He communicated to her that everything was going to be all right. And then her spirit came back into her body. Later, when I was in college, I interviewed two of the men who saw this happen to her. She was clammy and had no pulse, as if she had died. And it happened on the way to the car from a "cottage prayer meeting" held in a home. I've heard the story so many times. (I know some people may feel it borders on being a little "out there" and may find it unnerving, but I personally don't view it that way in light of the many stories put in print regarding out-of-body experiences.) I believe my mother genuinely had a powerful experience with God, and it made this whole thing of Jesus and heaven and the supernatural very real to me.

Then when I was twelve, doctors discovered that my Sunday school teacher had a large tumor about the size of those old foot-washing basins or, put another way, the size of one of those round watermelons. It was very serious, so everyone in our little Baptist church (I grew up Baptist) was praying for her. And I remember when the doctors did the operation, they went in and opened her up and found that the tumor had no roots connected to anything. It also had shrunk down to the size of a grapefruit, or actually an orange, and it just fell out of her body cavity.

All those healing events were registering in my childhood years, so healing was really real to me. But I had this kind of hang-up about it—some bad theology. I thought my grand-mother was one of the most saintly persons I'd ever met. She just worshiped all the time, in everything she did, and she was always listening to Christian radio. I didn't know till later that it was because she was illiterate. And my Sunday school teacher only had a second-grade education, but I thought she loved Jesus more than anyone else I knew, other than my grandma. So my view was that if you're saintly—really, really close to God—there's a chance you might get healed.

Then when I was sixteen, my maternal grandfather, whom I used to sit with in the "Amen corner" in the little Baptist church—my grandma's in the Shouting corner, my grandpa's in the Amen corner—he contracted cancer of the prostate. It had gone into his other organs and into his bones. And I would pray for him and rub him; he was in a lot of pain! He had a colostomy, but he didn't last. He died when he was 62 years old. We had asked the same people who prayed for my Sunday school teacher to pray for Grandpa, so when he died, that was a real discouragement. It confused me about healing.

At sixteen, I didn't know how to reconcile those two different stories in my own family about Grandpa and Grandma. By eighteen, I was backslidden. When I began to leave the Lord, I knew I would want to come back—I just wanted to go visit the prodigal land for a while. So I still came to church, but I was a hypocrite. I didn't want to get out of church entirely—I was afraid that if I didn't stay in church, I'd get so deeply involved in sin that I wouldn't be able to come "home." That explains some of the hypocrisy going on in my life at the time, but after eleven months I couldn't stand it anymore. I came back to the Lord, and I was rededicated on a Sunday night.

The following Thursday, October 15, 1970, I was almost killed in a car wreck. My second-best friend, who was sitting right beside me, was killed. His sister was seriously injured, and I had major injuries. I had sixty stitches in my face, three places the size of a quarter were totally crushed at my hairline, and if you rubbed your fingers across my forehead, there were so many cracks that it felt like a washboard. Some pieces of bone were gone, just missing entirely. One jaw was badly messed up, and the doctor said it had to be set. The cheekbone on that side was all crushed, my ribs were broke and I had a 10 to 15 percent compression in the thoracic vertebrae and disc area. It felt as if I had a three-inch knife blade sticking into me. My intestinal track was also paralyzed, my kidneys weren't working and there was blood in my urine. They had a tube pump in my stomach, and I had a catheter. They gave me 50 milligrams of Demerol every three hours. It put me to sleep. As soon as I'd wake up, I'd start begging for the next shot because I hurt so badly.

Now, I was eighteen, I'd just come back to the Lord, I'd been a backslidden hypocrite and I knew I wasn't a saintly person like my grandma and my Sunday school teacher. Yet we were going to have an evangelistic series of meetings in a month, and we called them "revival meetings" even though most times they weren't revival in the true sense of the word. (True revival is characterized by an unusual presence of God that attracts people to the Lord, with many conversions as a result of a deep conviction for sin. Most of the "revival" meetings we had were really planned evangelistic events, sometimes with gimmicks like "pack a pew" night.)

I didn't know the full extent of my injuries. I didn't know they had told my mother and dad I would be in the hospital from 49–77 days, and I didn't know how seriously I was hurt. I didn't know that after you suffer a major spinal injury, for several days the spinal cord can still swell so that even if you are not paralyzed at first, you can still become paralyzed. I didn't know all that. All they told me was that I couldn't even have a pillow, and they said, "Whatever you do, don't move! Don't bend your back! Don't try to get up!" If I needed anything, three nurses would come in and do a log roll, making sure my back didn't move or twist.

In the midst of that, my great-uncle, who was a Pentecostal preacher, came to the hospital to see me and pray for me. And my pastor prayed for me; lots of people were praying for me. I was in and out of consciousness the first three or four days. When I came to and was able to stay conscious, I told everyone, "I'm going to be at that revival." That was 28 days away, and the doctor had said I would be hospitalized a minimum of 49 days, and probably a lot longer. I could tell they all thought, *Yeah, sure you will. . . .*

I knew they didn't believe me, but for some reason I just believed that I would be at that revival. The first thing that happened was that since my intestinal tract wasn't working, they were going to transfer me to Barnes Hospital, the biggest one in St. Louis, to see if they could fix it. My church youth group prayed for me the night before and felt as though God had given them the assurance that I would be all right. When the doctors examined me the next morning, my intestines were working fine, so they pulled the tube out. But I wasn't connecting this to healing yet, I wasn't connecting the dots—I was just grateful to get that thing out of my nose!

Then a specialist came in to set my jaw. He looked at it and said, "Put your teeth together." Then he said, "Do it again! Again!" He checked it four times and said, "I don't understand this. I came here to set your jaw, and it's already set." Now when he said that, I connected the dots this time and said, "Oh, the Lord's healing me."

And then a third thing happened. I was still taking the Demerol every three hours for pain, but I couldn't take it in my arms anymore, so they just gave me shots in my thighs. When I woke up one morning, though, I just didn't have any pain. This was maybe fifteen days into it, and the pain was gone!

I still couldn't move around since they'd warned me not to, so my dad asked me what I could do while I was in the hospital. I said, "Bring me a Bible." Even though I had gone to church as a kid, I really hadn't read the Bible very much myself, so I started reading Genesis and Exodus and almost all of the New Testament. As I read about Jesus, I fell in love with Him in a new way. And the Bible was so alive.

I remember reading this one passage: "For what is your life? It is even a vapor that appears for a little time and then vanishes away" (James 4:14 NKJV). I marked it and thought, *Now, that's the truth.* Even though I thought I would live, at one point my life did flash in front of me and I thought, *Wow, it was so short!* I had accomplished a lot; I'd been freshman class president and junior year student leader, I'd been in sports and everything. And I thought, *None of that matters. The only thing that really matters is what I've done for Jesus and with Jesus.* Then they brought me pictures of the car we were in, and I thought, *It's a miracle anybody lived through that.* After I'd seen the pictures, I prayed one night, "Lord, You spared my life—I give it back to You. I'll do anything You want." And I added, "But I don't want to preach."

At sixteen, when I was first saved, I'd felt that maybe God was calling me to preach, but I'd tried to ignore that. I was afraid that if I became a preacher, I might backslide and have it affect all the people I had influence on. I was afraid I wouldn't be strong enough; that was really the only thing holding me back.

Lying there in bed after God healed me in those three ways I talked about, I got this strong impression, "Sit up in bed." And I thought, *Lord, they told me if I move at all, I could be paralyzed.*

**Bill:** Were you recognizing this impression as from the Lord?

**Randy:** Yes, even though I had never had any experience with that type or intensity of impression. But I did it; I sat up. The next impression came: "Put the bar down on the hospital bed." So I did that, and then the next impression was "Stand up."

I thought, *This better be You, Lord!* I was so convinced that it was God that I risked paralysis to follow the impressions. I put my feet over the bed and stood up. I closed the air-conditioning in my gown behind me and walked out into the aisle.

The nurses went crazy! "Hey! Get back in bed! You're not even supposed to move—we told you that you could be paralyzed!"

I wouldn't stay in bed, though. I kept getting out of bed, and I stopped wearing the air-conditioned gown. I had a friend bring me some clothes. I told the medical staff, "God has healed me. Let me go home."

They answered, "No, we need to get you a brace first, and you can't lift anything over ten pounds for the next year." Just a few months later, however, I was working in the oil fields again. I was completely healed.

Out of that healing after my accident came this renewed interest in healing. I got called to preach right after that, and then I started college in mid-January. The first day—this really should have been a clue for me—I went to the bookstore to buy textbooks, and the Bible I was supposed to use couldn't be the translation I already had. I was supposed to have a different translation. While I was in the bookstore, I heard this impression from God that I've never forgotten. It was, *The issue of your lifetime will be the Holy Spirit.*

That's an unusual word for a General Baptist to get. More like Assemblies of God or Church of God, Cleveland, or Pentecostal Holiness, sure, but for a General Baptist to get that was odd. It set me on a course, though, so that every time I could take a class that dealt with Pentecostalism or the charismatic movement or the Holy Spirit or the book of Acts—anything I could move toward along those lines—I would take the class and study because I knew God had told me that the issue of my lifetime would be that specific area.

Tragically, my college was so liberal that it destroyed much of my faith and all of my fire. The only thing that kept me from losing my Christian faith altogether in that liberal college environment was that I could never doubt my own healing. My healing was the salvation of my Christian faith. If I hadn't had that, I don't think I'd be in ministry today. I'd probably be an agnostic who embraces all these liberal arguments and hasn't seen God's power personally. Even though I was aware of my grandma's experience and all that, I needed to experience it myself.

When I got out of college, I realized that I didn't even believe enough to stay in the ministry. I decided to go to seminary and play the devil's advocate, trying to get answers to the very difficult questions that had been raised in my mind by my liberal college professors. In seminary, I took a class on the book of Acts. We could choose from fifty subjects as the topic of a term paper, and I told my professor, "I want to write on healing, but it's not on the list." Isn't it ironic that the whole course was on the book of Acts, and healing was not even one of the fifty options? Nothing about signs and wonders or anything like that! So I asked the professor, "Will you give me a special dispensation to write on healing?"

I got permission and wrote this paper that I still have. I just happened to find it two nights before this interview. On it, the professor commented, "You wrote as if healing is central to the Gospel. It's not, it's only peripheral. And if you continue to take this strong view about healing, it's going to get you in trouble in the Baptist church."

That proved true! But as I reread that paper and his comments now, I realize that today I'm more convinced than ever of the centrality of healing to the Gospel—more convinced than I was even back then. That whole incident built in me a foundation for healing because my professor had told me, "You can write on healing, but you can't use any anecdotal stories. You can't tell any personal stories. You have to research the topic."

After a lot of looking, I found a book by Morton Kelsey that really did teach me about healing and how it continued through the whole history of the Church. And that book was just the beginning. Later, after I got out of seminary, I read a book by Francis MacNutt on it. I was still intrigued by healing.

The major thing that sealed it all for me happened when I was 32 years old. I'd been in the ministry since I was 18, so about 14 years, and I had invited a young man of 20 or 21 to preach. He was attending the same college I'd gone to, and since

I was leaving on vacation the next day, he was preaching for me. On Sunday night I was listening to him, and he was doing the same thing I'd done many times, spiritualizing the story of the woman with the issue of blood. He gave it an application that had nothing to do with healing. I'd done the same myself. But what got my attention was that, even though I was thinking his sermon was just so-so, all of a sudden I started tearing up. The tears weren't gushing, but it felt as if they were shooting out, they were flowing so rapidly. *What's going on?* I thought. *It has nothing to do with what he's saying—it's not that good a sermon.*

He wasn't saying anything about healing, and it got to me all of a sudden. And I can still tell you today the impression I got from God. He said, *I want you to teach that I still heal today. I want you to hold a conference or seminar in this church on healing, and I want you to preach differently. No more three points and a poem. I want you to use a lot more of My words and a lot fewer of yours.* He even gave me the specifics: *I want you to do a series of sermons on the message and ministry or words and works of Jesus through the gospels. Just put them all together, make them one chronological history.*

I felt that I could teach through that in about six months. That was a hugely important moment because it set things in motion for the future. That night I went home and called a friend who did his doctoral dissertation at Southern Baptist Seminary in Louisville, where I'd gone. When I was writing my term paper on the Holy Spirit, he was writing his doctoral dissertation on a critique of American Pentecostal theology. His name was Dr. Larry Hart. I called to ask some questions, and I said, "Larry, you're one of the few people I know who believes in these things." I really didn't know anyone else other than my great-uncle, and he was far too legalistic for me. I admired certain things about him, but there were other things about his expression that just didn't attract me. There was a little bit of pride in him; he'd put my grandpa down and say, "When the Rapture comes, you're not going to make it. You're going to go about six feet up and come back down because you smoke cigarettes." So I didn't want to ask him a lot of questions; I asked Larry instead. I said, "I'd like you or Francis MacNutt or Morton Kelsey to come help me here." I didn't know enough about Morton Kelsey to know that he probably wouldn't have been a good choice because it turned out later that I didn't agree with his emphasis on Jungian psychology, but I wanted Larry or Francis MacNutt.

Larry said, "Yeah, I'll come—I'm glad to come. But I've heard everybody at Oral Roberts University who deals with healing, almost everybody you can think of, and there's this one man. If you could get *him* to come, he's the best person I've ever heard in activating laypeople in healing."

"Who's that?" I wanted to know.

"John Wimber."

"I've never heard of John Wimber, and I don't want to invite someone in I've never heard of."

Larry said, "If you want me, I'll come. But just think about it; pray about it."

The next day I started my vacation. I was going through the house and we had Christian TV turned on. We had a satellite of TBN with Paul Crouch and Trinity Network, and I was walking by the set, not even planning to listen, but I picked up on something that was being said. I sat down on the couch a minute to watch, and I was intrigued. This guy didn't act like most guys who were usually on. He had a different style, and I sat there the whole hour and listened to him. *I don't know who that guy is,* I thought, *but what he just said is what I believe. I just didn't have the words to say it. Who is this guy? He looks like Kenny Rogers and Santa Claus rolled into one.*

Right after that, Paul Crouch said, "It's been our privilege to have John Wimber on with us today."

I thought, *This is not an accident; this is a divine appointment!*

So I taped the rerun in the afternoon, took it to the deacons at church and said, "I want to invite this guy to come to our Baptist church." I didn't know he wouldn't come to a little village church of 150, so I called him and asked him if he would.

He said, "I can't come myself, but I could send you a team."

I agreed. I thought, *Okay, if you can't come, I'll take a team.* That is the smartest thing I ever did. A lot of people ask me to come now, too. If I can't come, I tell them, "But I recommend a team." And most of the time they say no—and that is really dumb. The smartest thing I did was have Wimber's team come because here's a truth: The team under someone carries that person's anointing.

It took me about six months to get my church ready by preaching through that material the Lord had highlighted in the impression He gave me. I taught my church things about the gifts of the Spirit and got them ready so that when Wimber's team came, they'd have a place to hang what they were bringing. Then they came, one preacher and four laypeople. We were a Baptist church having a conference conducted by a key Vineyard leader and a team from the Vineyard, and we had the most powerful meeting Wimber said they had ever had in the United States. Actually, he wrote about a Baptist church in his book *Power Evangelism* (Harper & Row, 1986), and it was my church!

I saw the blind see, the deaf hear. I saw myself, my people and my wife get touched. My wife, DeAnne, was bitter and hurt. Her dad had just died of alcoholic sclerosis of the liver, and she had severe TMJD (temporomandibular joint disorder).

God healed her physically. She couldn't get certain memories out of her mind, and God healed her emotionally.

I got the first baptism of the Spirit with power that I'd ever had. I'd already spoken in tongues for years, since I was 19, but now I was 32. I felt as though I were being electrocuted. I just shook, and the next day all my joints ached. And I'd never prayed for anybody and had them fall down in my life. But for months after that, I'd pray for people and they'd fall down. I'd also get these words of knowledge.

**Bill:** This is all in the Baptist church?

**Randy:** This is in the Baptist church. I had laypeople getting more words of knowledge and seeing extravagant, precise, bizarre open visions. They were seeing angels and demons and discerning spirits. I didn't move in any of the seeing areas of revelation. But the big, big thing for me—because I had become so desperate for more—was hearing that impression from God as that young college guy was preaching. He was spiritualizing one of the gospel stories of healing, but as I said, God so clearly told me that I was to teach that *He still heals today.*

I had already begun to do that, actually, but then something had happened that got in my way. Maybe twelve or eighteen months before, I had begun preaching a series on MacNutt's book *Healing* in my Baptist church. And I didn't just preach it; I prayed for the sick. Then a woman faked a healing, and I didn't know she was faking. I got caught up in it and had her give her testimony many times. And then she had another issue and I prayed for her, and this time I had a check in my spirit that something was not right. I began to investigate and realized that I had been duped. I felt so embarrassed about not having good discernment and making claims that weren't true. I was so frustrated by that situation that I wouldn't pray for anybody, yet I was so desperate to learn more. I hadn't prayed for one soul for eighteen months until that night when I heard the Lord say, *You teach that I still heal today.*

And so we did have the conference with Wimber's team, and I did teach that series. And out of that conference my life was set in motion. I went to see Wimber. He heard the Lord say to him that I would be one of the two guys in the Vineyard movement who would go around the world and lay hands on people for activation of the gifts of the Spirit. Wimber didn't tell me that until right before he died, but his associate let it slip accidentally, so I knew it before then. But it was ten years between the time he heard that for the first time and the time he called me and said, "What God showed me about you now starts." It took from January 1984 to January 1994.

From that point on in my Baptist church in 1984, my interest in healing only increased to where it is today. That event in my Baptist church, when there was a special call for me to really teach and preach on healing, was how I really knew that I was called in that area. And once I saw the way Blaine Cook, Wimber's team leader, gave an invitation, I've done it the same ever since. (He'd say, "I don't want you to come to the front just because you want to be touched. I don't want you to come forward unless you begin to feel the love of God so strong you have tears—the power of God so strong your hands are trembling or electrified—the glory so strong it becomes difficult to stand up straight. Your hands may begin to feel as if they have fallen asleep and are waking up. If any of these things happen, I want you to come to the front for prayer. I believe God wants to touch and bless everyone, but there are some whom He wants to give gifts of healing to.") For 26 years I've given that same invitation he did, because I saw how it worked and I have faith for it. So I've never backed away from healing since March of 1984.

**Bill:** That's all amazing. Back when you were in the hospital after your accident and you got prayed for, did you feel anything?

**Randy:** The youth group wasn't with me. They prayed at the church, quite a long distance away.

**Bill:** Oh, they prayed long-distance? And they felt a witness?

**Randy:** Yes, they had a peace. They actually came to visit me the next day and said, "It was really weird. The door at church was open that's usually locked, and the altar lights were on." It was actually kind of spooky to them. They told each other, "This is weird!" And they said that there was such a presence that when they all prayed, really concerned for my life at one point, they absolutely felt, *He's going to be all right.* So when I told them the next day that the tube was taken out and my digestive tract was fine, you can imagine their reaction.

**Bill:** You mentioned that a number of folks in the church were getting better, more precise words of knowledge and that God was using them even more than He was using you. What was that like for you?

**Randy:** That was scary. I was insecure because I thought, *I'm the pastor. I should be seen as one of the more spiritual persons in the church. And if there are other laypeople moving more powerfully in these gifts than I am, they'll lose respect for me.*

I was worried about that. Really early on, I'd snuck off to an Assembly of God church and just sat on the back row watching. I watched people fall, and I wasn't even sure I believed in it. I didn't believe in it until I saw people falling who I know wouldn't do that. But at least I'd seen it before. None of the people in my church had even been to a Pentecostal church, so we had no grid for any of these things that were happening. We didn't know there could be catchers. We'd never heard of getting drunk in the Spirit, yet we had people who needed to be driven home at midnight because they were so drunk in the Spirit that they couldn't drive. All the things that happened the sixty days I was in Toronto (at the start of the Toronto Blessing) were things I'd already seen happen in my Baptist church ten years earlier.

But the threatening thing was, this one guy named John had such a gift of discernment, and he'd go into open visions and he'd know things about people before he'd meet them. I was struggling with that. And I had a special ed school teacher, my associate pastor's wife, who would see words on people. And her husband, a coal miner, would go into open visions and get great detail. And we saw major healings. A little boy was dying of a major disease, and my associate pastor saw a vision about it. We didn't even know how to interpret it; we just gave it, and the boy got healed. I couldn't see angels, I couldn't see demons, and I had people who could do that. It was just visitation.

I felt threatened because I didn't experience any of that. I just felt people's pain. So one day while we were driving down the road, I told my wife, DeAnne, "I don't like this. I don't like these people being more anointed, more gifted than me. It makes me feel insecure. Why would God do that?"

DeAnne gave me some really good advice. She said, "Randy, think about a few things. First, if you could do everything, you wouldn't need any of us. Second, if you could do everything, you could get proud. And third, you're still the pastor of this church, and these gifts are just gifts. You have to pastor the persons with the gifts. You have to help them mature. If they're not pastored well, they could self-destruct."

That was true, it really was true. And it gave me a peace. I came to a place with the Lord where I could say, "I'll cherish every person and every gift You give us, because it's going to make the church stronger. It's good, and I thank You for the opportunity to pastor these people and help them mature and grow in the Lord."

**Bill:** It's interesting to hear about how you started out feeling threatened by other people's gifts and contrast that with how you live now. I've hung out with you for ten or twelve years, maybe thirteen, and I've observed how you celebrate people and their gifts so strongly. Not just their gifts, but their uniqueness, wherever they operate differently from you, and how they see or feel or pick up on things differently from you. It's quite a change. When did that start? Was it after your wife's counsel?

**Randy:** As soon as my wife told me that, I was totally set free. Instead of feeling threatened, I started celebrating. It's interesting that you're asking these questions, because the only other time I can think of that I really felt intimidated by another person's gift was when I first came to your church. I had a young man named Ben Scofield with me. I had just taught at a sister church in St. Louis, and Ben had come up to me there and said, "I'm sick; I'm nauseous." And I began to pray for him, but then I said, "Wait a minute—when did you begin to get nauseous?"

He said, "When you started teaching about words of knowledge."

I said, "Ben, you're not sick. You're having a word of knowledge." He had been backslidden himself until recently, and he was only eighteen years old. And I said, "Hey, everybody, Ben's got a word of knowledge. Who's sick and feeling nauseous?"

Two people raised their hands, so I said to them, "Come here." Then I said, "Ben, you're going to pray for them."

Ben had never prayed for anybody like that, but he said later, "I remembered how you'd prayed for me, and I tried to do just what you did to me."

The nauseous people got healed. Then Ben had another word; he had three or four that night. He'd give them and pray for the people, then he'd get more words, and they were more specific.

I asked Ben to travel with me. He's the only person I've ever asked to travel with me at my expense. He traveled with me for two years, and I put about $60,000 into him. He got to a point where he'd be driving down the road in a car and somebody would pull up beside him and he'd have a word of knowledge. The way he'd know it was for them was that when they pulled away and got ahead of him, the pain would leave. Then when he'd catch up to them, the pain would come back.

Even before I knew stuff like that, I was so impressed with him that I asked him to travel with me, like I said. But I made a mistake—I forgot to ask his dad's permission first. So I had to apologize to his dad and ask him if it was okay.

"As long as you make him work for it," his dad told me. "I don't want him just traveling with you; I want him to develop a work ethic and have a servant heart."

So that was our agreement. The first time Ben went with me—that was to your church—I'd had several words of knowledge, maybe five or six. Then I said, "Ben, do you have a word of knowledge?"

"I think I do," he said, even though it was his first time out.

He was the first intern I'd ever had, and I felt as though he was a spiritual son. I was going to train him. So when he said, "I think I have one," and he gave it, I was so proud. And he gave another word, and I was proud. And he gave another, and my buttons were about to pop off—he'd only been with me a week! *Look at how God is using my intern*, I thought. Then he'd had as many words as I'd had, five or six. Then he had seven, eight, nine, ten. . . . I mean, I was getting a little nervous. I could actually feel myself distancing from him. And I was getting uncomfortable and thinking, *Wait a minute, I'm supposed to be his mentor. He's my disciple. He's already had twice as many words as I've had. That makes me look bad.* I was actually feeling things that I didn't like and getting uneasy. He'd had four times as many words as I'd had, like fifteen or twenty.

**Bill:** Yeah, I remember that!

**Randy:** It was unbelievable! And in that moment, the second thing happened that really changed me in this area. The Holy Spirit spoke. Ben was the same age as my oldest son, and the Holy Spirit said, *Do you want Ben to be your spiritual son?*
I said, "Yes."
The Holy Spirit said, *If he were your biological son, would you be threatened now? Or would you be proud, and would you be delighted and excited that your son has gone past you?*
I said, "I'd be so happy!" And in that one moment, the revelation came that to be a real spiritual father, I needed to have that kind of response. Now, Will or Jamie or Timothy or Ben or any of my interns and their gifts don't threaten me. I really want them to do more, accomplish more. And I can brag on them and not feel threatened. They may surpass me—and I want them to!

**Bill:** That's amazing!

# 8

# LAUNCHED INTO INCREASE

**Bill:** What kind of experiences have you had in praying for healing, Randy, that have really expanded you and caused you to grow? What kind of things have launched you?

**Randy:** The initial thing was the anointing I received when Blaine prayed for me in the Baptist church, when Wimber sent him under Vineyard. That was my initial launch. Learning how to receive and recognize words of knowledge was another major thing that caused an increase. Then there was an increase for impartation. That one happened after the Lord asked me to go on a 40-day fast. I don't fast, hardly ever. But there was a season in my life when I fasted for 21 days, 21, 14, 14 and 40. And then after that 40 days, I didn't fast again for 10 years, not even for one day if I can remember correctly. But that fast was for more anointing in the Holy Spirit, more healing and more power.

That was in early 1984. Then 1994 came around, and I saw so many children who needed not just healings—they needed creative miracles. The number of healings was greatly increasing, but with the increase, faith was increasing on the part of parents. They started pulling their kids out of institutions and bringing them for healing. One little girl was blind. One boy suffered massive brain damage. He'd been normal until he was sixteen, but now he was spastic and couldn't talk. Another girl had Parkinson's disease at twelve years old, and another boy of about twelve had spina bifida and was in a wheelchair. His sister had cerebral palsy, and they were both adopted. I saw all of them within six months, and it caused me to go on another forty-day fast ten years after the first one. It was the only other time I went on a forty-day fast, and it was for a breakthrough in creative miracles. I knew what I was fasting for. I can't fast without it being unto something and without feeling that God has led me to it. I'm just not a disciplined person. I admire people who are so disciplined that every Monday or Tuesday or Wednesday they fast. I admire that—I just don't have the grace to do it. But on the twenty-third day of my second forty-day fast, I saw my first creative miracle. (A woman was healed of advanced Parkinson's disease.) There was increase after that.

Not quite a year later, in January 1995, I went to Melbourne, Florida, to do a meeting. God came there, and the meetings continued for eight and a half months, six nights a week. I was there in January first, and I worked on and off for four weeks with the pastors until they could carry the revival. I was also in Charlotte, North Carolina, that same month, January 1995, and I saw more miracles in that time than I had seen in the first 24 years put together! I can't attribute that breakthrough to anything specific. It wasn't that anybody gave me an insight or that I got a revelation. It wasn't a new truth; it wasn't that I had fasted and sought it. The only thing I can attribute it to was that for 24 years I had been knocking on the door of healing, and God came. I can't say anything else other than that, but it was a major breakthrough.

I've told you about the top things that have really caused breakthroughs in my life, but there's another one I want to mention. It was going to Latin America and meeting Omar Cabrera. I learned a lot about healing by working with him and watching how he did things. I thought the anointing on my life there was just because I was in Argentina. I was with Pablo Bottari, and Victor Lorenzo was coming up, and we'd had all these healings, more than I'd ever seen in the United States. The United States was a lot different back then. Real breakthrough has come in the United States, but back then it was really dry and there was so much skepticism. I wasn't seeing much in the United States, though we'd seen a lot in that January meeting. So while I was in Argentina, I was walking down the sidewalk and saying, "Man, I've come under the anointing of revival in Argentina. We're seeing so many people get healed; it must be because I'm here."

And Victor Lorenzo said, "No, Randy, that's not true. What we just saw happen in your life, I've seen it happen in Claudio Freidzon, Carlos Annacondia, Omar Cabrera. . . ." He named several men who have become famous now, but back then God hadn't lifted them up yet. And he went on, "It's not that you're here. There is something on you."

That really encouraged me. And then Omar Jr. said on the way home, "You know, Randy, you have an anointing similar to my father. And if I had what you have, I would do what he's done." And he told me what he would do (hold healing meetings in cities on a monthly basis to build enough people to begin churches). But the Lord never told me to do that.

These are the things that have helped me. The other thing that caused a major breakthrough has been you. I'm not saying that because you're sitting across from me, Bill. It's true. We've influenced each other a lot.

A little over a year ago, when you and I were at the Revival Alliance meeting in Maui, we'd been telling all these healing stories. Right before we left you said to me, "Wait a minute, I forgot to tell you that I've seen thirty or more people healed who had metal in their bodies."

I couldn't believe it. I thought, *How could you forget to tell me this?*

You said, "I don't know if the metal is disappearing, but I do know that what they could not do before because of the metal, they now can do. I don't know if the metal is gone or if it's just changing. I can't understand it, but it's happening."

I got so excited when you said that. I thought, *If that's what God's doing, I want in on it.* So at the next meeting I went to after you told me that, I got up and said, "I just found out from Bill Johnson that God is healing people with metal in their bodies, so we're going to go for it. How many people have metal here? Stand up."

People stood up and I prayed, and nobody got healed. It was devastating. I was really expecting somebody to get healed.

**Bill:** Wow. Even though problems with metal weren't healed, were there many other miracles in that room?

**Randy:** Yes, there were other healings in the meeting. Not metal healings, as I said, but just kind of the normal other stuff. But the metal healings—I was really expecting those, and they didn't happen. So I told myself, *That really knocked the faith out of you to expect that; you better wait awhile before you try again.* So I decided I would wait and maybe see you again first.

Before this, you and I both had been with James Maloney in England, and you'd told me that James was the one you'd heard about praying for metal first. And he had this anointing, so you and I both asked him to pray for us. So the impartation happened in your life.

**Bill:** At that time it was well over two hundred documented cases that he had seen.

**Randy:** Right. It started happening in your life, so I thought, *Well, it worked for Bill, but it didn't work for me.* I went to Loveland, Colorado, next, and this is how we got a breakthrough. It really affected me and increased my faith. I had already determined that I wasn't going to pray for metal, but as I was getting ready to eat, this guy gave me a folded-up paper and said, "Look at this. I'm in excruciating pain."

I unfolded the paper, which was a cervical X-ray of his neck. I counted the screws in his neck—he had 23 or 24, maybe more, I forget now. And four rods around his spine and crossbars, too. I thought, *How in the world can that be? No wonder he's in pain!* Then I decided, *I'm not going to go for that. It didn't work last time.*

Tonya, my daughter-in-law, handed me the order of service, so I got ready to go in. A guy named Jim just happened to be there, and I knew he had seen metal disappear. He was a friend of healing evangelist Leif Hetland (whom I've laid hands on and prophesied over). Since he was right there, I thought, *Well, okay.* . . . And then I thought again, *I'm not going to do it. I am not going to do this!*

The worship ended, and I did it. I said, "I found out God is healing people with metal in their bodies. Everyone with metal stand up."

Forty-seven people with metal stood up, and we prayed. Jim prayed, and I prayed and we included the guy with all the screws. Twenty-three people were healed. Eleven of them came up and gave their testimony. The next day I interviewed five or six of them for several hours. They had been on morphine patches, morphine drips, Percocet, you name it—these people had suffered years of excruciating pain. And we saw them doing things they could not do before. It blew my mind.

From that day on, for a year, I counted up everybody who came up and gave a testimony about that kind of healing—just those. That doesn't even count the ones who raised their hands to say they were healed. We counted 180 people who testified that they were healed of issues having to do with metal in their bodies. And it's happened here; even tonight we had a testimony of that. So now it's probably over 200 in fourteen months. That breakthrough happened because of iron sharpening iron and you telling me that God was doing that. It gave me faith to try it. (As of December 2011, we have over 400 testimonies of people with metal in their bodies being healed.)

That was one thing you told me that brought breakthrough, but there was a second thing you said just a few months ago. I don't know if you can remember, but you pulled me aside and said, "Randy, you need to go for more than you're going for," or something like that. I'm paraphrasing, and maybe you can tell me exactly what you said. I remember something about, "You need to believe that you can just pronounce healings and don't always need to pray for them. And if you can just get people up and get them to do something, then they'll be healed just by your word."

Not only did you tell me that, but I watched you do it several times yourself. I've been studying you and thinking, *He didn't used to do this. Bill's growing.*

It's kind of like if you see two runners and one picks up the pace, then that helps the other one. Like my dad said about training horses—if you take one horse that's got a good gait and take one that doesn't and put them together, the good one will develop the other one. That's how you can train horses. I feel as though God sometimes does that to us. He puts us together so each of us will learn from the other one.

I was at High Point, North Carolina, in February this year, after you told me that in January sometime, and I started getting these words of knowledge. Instead of doing what I normally do, having people stand up and then praying for them, I didn't pray. I just said the next thing that came into my head after they stood. It was something that would make sense for them to try; I wouldn't say something like "Go row a boat" or anything. But maybe they had a knee problem, and I'd say, "Bend your knee like that, five times." Then another word would come right after it, stronger, and I'd go for that one the same way.

It didn't make sense to me, but I was so excited that I was like a kid in a candy store. I actually brought the video home to the Global School of Supernatural Ministry and said, "I want you guys to watch what I just learned this week." I told them the story of what you said to me and how we went for it. As I showed them the video, I tried to explain the whole process I was going through in that service. "This is what I was thinking when I did that," I told them, "and this is what I was thinking when I said that. . . ."

So in the last year, those two things you spoke to me about—that God was healing people with metal and that I needed to go for more and just get people up doing something they couldn't do before—those two things really brought breakthrough. But the thing that caused the greatest breakthrough for me was your encouragement.

**Bill:** That's amazing. In this last instance, when you had people bend their legs five times or whatever you told them, did you do that just randomly with whomever you called out a word of knowledge for? Or did you wait to see something specific on them?

**Randy:** No, I just told them all to do whatever it was.

**Bill:** Everybody? That's interesting.

**Randy:** Everybody. I just said, "All of you do that," because usually there were three to seven people each time. One time, everybody got healed except two, and they eventually got healed. One of the two who didn't get healed had an issue with her tailbone. When I gave that word of knowledge, I told everyone who responded to sit down three times, and many got healed right then, but she didn't. When she sat down three times, it didn't work. I asked her, "What about you?"
She said, "I'm the same."
I said, "Do it again—but sit down hard."
She did it, and right away she said, "I'm healed."
The other person who wasn't healed had a problem with her lower lumbar disc area, and she didn't have any teeth, either. Someone had paid her way to come through a scholarship. She was very, very poor. I could tell by talking to her that she had a lot of self-image problems related to her station in life. I could tell she'd lived a hard life, and I felt God's compassion for her. I felt that God wanted to heal her, but there are times when you've got the service going and you can't spend too much time with one person. This was not a moment when I was praying for the sick, this was when I was just giving words of knowledge, and we needed to take up the offering. But I walked over to her and found out that her last lumbar above her tailbone was totally destroyed. Totally disintegrated. It had a bunch of screws in it, but the doctors couldn't even rebuild it. She was in terrible pain.

I felt such compassion and I felt God was going to heal her, but I knew it would take a little longer than what we really had time to do in the service right then. God had a lot more He wanted to do that we also needed to attend to. So while an associate took up the offering, I sat down by this lady on the front row and put my hand on her back. I didn't pray; I just said, "I believe the Lord is going to heal you as we sit here. We're going to give this more time." And I asked, "Are you sensing anything?"

"Yes, my back is really hot," she answered.

"That's good!" I said.

God was releasing healing in her back. I knew He would, and I knew I needed to take that little bit of extra time with her. But by the time the offering was over and we'd gotten through some of the announcements and stuff, she was healed.

Sometimes I may have ten or twenty words of knowledge before I get up to give them. Sometimes I don't have any beforehand, and God will give them to me when I get up there. But one of the other things I've learned is that sometimes one of the words that comes is so unique, so much stronger than the others, that I have an impression that God will use it to break faith out in the room. So for that one word—and I won't do this for any of the other ones—I'll say, "All of you who have this condition, I want you to come down here right in front of everybody." And often I'll give the word first, before I do anything else. I've learned that usually when it's really strong, either a lot of people will have it or it will be a very severe kind of problem that will be a faith builder. Almost everyone will get healed really quickly when that happens. So sometimes I do make a distinction between the different words that come and how I give them, and other times things don't happen that way, so I don't do that.

# 9

# REACHING NEW REALMS

**Bill:** I'm still curious about the metal healings you've seen, Randy. As I understand it, none of the times when people with metal were healed involved words of knowledge.

**Randy:** Never. I've never had a word of knowledge about metal to this day—or at least until yesterday. Yesterday a word of knowledge about metal came, and I didn't even know it was a word. Then that woman came back tonight and gave a testimony about it. I'll get to her story in a minute. But my point is, I almost never give words of knowledge about metal—the healings come just by the faithfulness of God.

**Bill:** Explain what you mean by that, Randy, because that's a big deal. If you're accustomed to ministering out of words of knowledge and you start shifting to another realm, what is it?

**Randy:** What I began to see was that every time I said, "God is going to heal people with metal," He did (except that first time).

As I've watched this—the consistency, the faithfulness, how it happened all the time—my faith has risen to where I realize that I have faith for this kind of healing that is not based on a word. A word of knowledge creates faith, but the faithfulness of God and seeing these healings happen so much has also created faith. Now I really don't need a word of knowledge to believe for it; I just need to say, "God is going to heal problems with metal."

I have to confess, though, that there's warfare over this. The enemy will say, "You know, you may become presumptuous over this."

I know that's not the Lord. I have to face that warfare, but I say, "No, God has been faithful! I'm going to go for it."

Sometimes it's even a battle in my mind beforehand, but I still go for it. And it's not because of a word of knowledge; it's because of the faithfulness of God. I have a faith for this kind of healing. I can actually say that if I were to go for it and nobody got healed of metal problems, I'd be shocked because I'm expecting it to happen.

I do have to correct myself. There was another time when it didn't happen. It was in a little church of about 120 where only one or two people had metal, and I was in Paris—not necessarily the land of faith. But apart from that, the metal healings have happened every time. And that's a major faith builder; this whole thing has been a real faith builder.

I don't know if I really answered your last question, though. I chased around a lot.

**Bill:** I was just asking what you're operating out of, what you're shifting to, when it's not a word of knowledge, and you described it very well. If I were to summarize your answer, I'd say you're operating in those situations out of the conviction of who you've seen God to be in a specific manifestation.

**Randy:** And sensing that it's almost like there's this area now where God says, "I'm going to give you this area."

**Bill:** Right, it's a realm.

**Randy:** Absolutely, it's a realm. And I don't have faith to do that with any other issues besides metal, except for one. I have faith like that for women who have had back injuries from pregnancy because I've seen those healed so often. But that area usually has to be quickened to my mind first. It doesn't necessarily take a word of knowledge; I just think of that area, and then I can go forward.

**Bill:** That's interesting because we've done the same with tailbone injuries during pregnancy. I think the healings are at 100 percent, or really close to 100 percent. Let me ask you another question.

**Randy:** Okay, but wait a minute. First, let me get back to the rabbit trail I was on at the start about the one word of knowledge I've gotten when it comes to metal, the one where I didn't know it was a word. Last night, I said to everyone—and this part didn't have anything to do with words of knowledge, I was just explaining to people—"You may have metal in your arm, you may have metal in your back, you may have metal in your knee. . . ." And people at the service told me that then I added, "You may have metal in your cervix."

Bill, you were there when I said it, and you know that doesn't even make sense. So when they told me about it, I replied, "I didn't say that!" But I guess I did. I didn't even know there *could* be metal in a cervix, but that was actually a word of knowledge.

(I later found out by watching the video that, just as I thought, I did not say *cervix*, but rather *cervical area*, referring to the neck. The woman who had metal in her cervix, however, did *hear* cervix, as did another woman next to her, who asked, "How could you have metal in the cervix?" I really said *cervical area*, yet God still healed the woman's cervix.)

I didn't know it was a word of knowledge; I thought I was just naming different places in the body where metal could be. But a girl actually had metal in her cervix, and she got healed! The metal disappeared, and she had it confirmed medically today. It disappeared—it's gone. It's not in her body anymore. And it was the type where it would have taken a C-section–type surgery to remove it.

The girl said that the doctors had told her they'd have to open her up and go in to remove the metal. It was a birth control device, and they had said before they ever put it in, "If you opt for this, you have to be sure you don't want any more kids!"

Somebody might think, *If she paid money to have that put in, you just messed her up, along with her husband.*

God did that. A month prior, a guy in her life group told this girl, "God told me you're going to have a son."

She told him, "You're crazy! I can't get pregnant." She knew her husband would have liked to have a son, though. And now she's excited about wanting to have a son. God made it a possibility.

**Bill:** How amazing. Have you used a breakthrough like this— not a word of knowledge, but a realm like we've been talking about—as a basis to get breakthrough in another realm? Have you ever seen that happen?

**Randy:** I did get a breakthrough in one realm, but it wasn't really connected to seeing a breakthrough in another. It was connected to a story—the testimony of Jesus. It happened when I was in my early fifties, and I've been in the ministry now for forty years. (I was eighteen when I preached my first sermon.)

I heard the testimony that God was raising the dead in Mozambique. I was in Brazil at the time and was praying for two stroke victims on the same night. I had never seen a stroke victim healed, ever. I didn't have faith for it, because I had prayed for quite a few stroke victims over the years as a pastor and had never seen a healing. This was an area I didn't have a lot of faith for. But I realized that I should no longer see it as hopeless because I started thinking, *God is raising the dead, all of whose brain cells have been destroyed—in fact, all the cells in their bodies! That's got to take resurrection power. If that's the case, then God can heal stroke victims, too!* So I had this new expectation that God can heal stroke victims.

That night in Brazil, we saw two stroke victims. They both had paralyzed arms; the right side of their brains had been affected, and their left sides were paralyzed. They had claw hands like you see with strokes, drawn up and useless. The woman couldn't talk, either. Her speech had been affected.

The man wasn't even saved, and the woman was Roman Catholic, but she had come to this Pentecostal church service. She still had a veil on and everything. It was amazing she was there at all; it's rare in Latin America since the two groups don't cross much.

Before the service started, we had about an hour of prayer where we prayed as a team, and then there was an hour of worship before I preached. Actually, we had two teams, and I was floating between the two. Both the stroke victims were prayed for. By the time I got up to start preaching, I saw the guy crying, and he had his hands raised up. He had been healed of the stroke. I looked at the woman, and she was clapping her hands and *singing* in worship. She had been healed of the stroke.

That was in Petropolis up in the mountains of Brazil. The next day, we come back down to Rio de Janeiro and saw a man in a wheelchair. He'd been confined to it for years from a stroke. That night, he got up and walked. So I went from no healings for strokes at all to this "first fruit" season, as I call it, where we had three healings in 24 hours. And that was connected to the testimony I heard about God raising the dead, which built my faith for that same resurrection power to heal stroke victims.

You've talked to me about experiencing this, Bill, where one thing leads to another. I'm paying attention to it now, more so since the last time I interviewed you a week or two ago. I'm believing it's going to happen more. You actually did something like that at tonight's service. You took one kind of healing and went into another. I watched you. See, I do watch you! When I first saw Rodney, it wasn't about healing, it was about impartation. But I remember Wimber or Blaine or probably both of them saying, "I can only do what I see the Father do." And they'd talk about it and ask, "Did you see the Spirit on it?"

I had no idea what they meant; I had to learn it along the way because I was a Baptist and I didn't understand the language of their group or this type of thing. I'd ask, "What do you mean, 'Did you see the Spirit?' Did you see an aura, a glow, a cloud, a pigeon, a dove? What do you mean, you saw the Spirit?"

And they'd answer, "We've learned how to see the effects of the Spirit on the human body, and we clue in to those things."

And I'd say, "Why didn't you say that? I understand that. But the other stuff is too mysterious."

I went to see Rodney in 1993, and he'd say to people, "There it is, take it." And I'd be thinking, *There is what? What did he just see?* So I followed him for a long time, until he made me quit. And I told myself, *I don't want to forget what I'm seeing.* I learn by what I see and by focusing on what I intentionally want to be imprinted on my mind. As I was watching him, I was praying, *God, I want to see in my life what I'm watching this man do!* And I carefully observed him and asked myself, *How is he flowing with God? What's he seeing? How is he getting these communications?*

When I first followed Wimber, I'd watch him and wonder the same thing: *What's he seeing?* I didn't travel with Wimber, but at first I would go to meet with him somewhere, and he'd tell me, "You come with me and be my shadow. You watch, and when we're done, if you have any questions, you ask and I'll explain things to you."

I thought he did this with everybody, but I found out later it was because he had heard that word about me when he first met me—that one day I would go around the world and lay hands on people. So he was actually sowing into me, and I didn't even know why. But the time he took to explain things to me was really, really encouraging.

Do you know I do that with you now, Bill? I watch you. Then when you and I talk together, I can ask questions and it really helps me put things together.

**Bill:** That's priceless how Wimber sowed into you and how you learned from asking him and others questions.

I'd like for you to address one of the things that I learned from *you* in the early days. I remember you mentioning that you were getting no breakthrough with things having to do with the head—the mind or the head.

**Randy:** I was referring to mental illness.

**Bill:** That's it, mental illness. So what you would do is target what you weren't seeing. You would target it in prayer for a season, and then you'd start getting a breakthrough. Following your lead, we tried doing the same thing, and we started getting breakthrough in areas that we previously weren't touching.

What I feel we're touching on here is that you would take a testimony, like the raising of the dead you just talked about, and use that as a springboard to give you a confidence to go into another realm of miracles. That's huge, because what we're seeing right now is so interconnected. In our creative miracle tonight, we had what appeared to be cartilage replaced in knees. And it's so much easier to pray for stuff that you can't see, like cartilage inside a knee, instead of a missing finger or that sort of thing. But if God is replacing missing cartilage, He can replace missing fingers. . . .

So using a realm that you already have breakthrough in to press into something new like that is just huge. And so is targeting unrealized areas, which I learned from you and your team way back at the beginning. I remember you talking when you first came to Redding about praying for specific things that way. Can you think of any more areas of healing you targeted in prayer that you started getting breakthrough in?

**Randy:** There were two. We finally did get a breakthrough in them after a seemingly heart-wrenching defeat at first. I had mentioned to you that my church in St. Louis was the only church in the city that had a support group for the mentally ill. You had to be certifiably diagnosed with a mental illness to be in this support group. I had laid hands on the guy who led it and prayed for him. He had been severely bipolar and got healed, so he was the group leader. For every year he had been on medicine, he had spent two weeks in the hospital's psych ward. The medicine wasn't controlling his problem.

After we prayed for him, he both lowered the amount of his medicine and never needed to be hospitalized again, as far as I know. That's been over thirty years ago. He's never been hospitalized since, except for one day when he voluntarily checked himself in. His wife had just found out she had breast cancer and needed a mastectomy. They also had a new baby. Stress can trigger things, and under the stress of all that, he thought, *Maybe I need to put myself in the hospital, just in case.* He was there one day and decided, *I didn't need to put myself in here!* So he checked himself out, and that was the end of it.

Because we had that group, all of a sudden we had all these people with mental illness issues in our church. I quickly became aware of how destructive it was. We were seeing quite a few physical healings at the time, but not mental illness healings—no bipolar, no schizophrenia, no clinical depression healings. No one else but this one group leader; he was the "first fruit" because he got healed the first time he came.

So I would open my Bible to Psalm 103:2–3: "Praise the LORD, O my soul, and forget not all his benefits—who forgives all your sins and heals all your diseases." I'd take my two associates with me, and the last thing we'd do before Sunday would come is walk through every aisle. It wasn't a big church, so it didn't take that long. We'd lay our hands on every chair and confess this passage of Scripture and say, "Lord, in our experience, we're not seeing this. But Your Word says that You heal us of all our diseases. So Lord, we're confessing this promise in Your Word, and we're asking for the anointing to come in this church. We're asking to begin seeing mental illness healed."

We prayed that for quite a while, and then we began to get a breakthrough. Then one of the guys, a schizophrenic I'd pray for anytime I saw him anywhere, even uptown, died from an accidental overdose. That was devastating. He was only twenty-something. It was a real blow. For me, schizophrenia was our

Goliath taunting the armies of Israel. Everything else was falling, but we still had this Goliath, and it was schizophrenia.

In Tucson, Arizona, though, we saw a young woman who was in the psych ward with schizophrenia 180 days a year. She couldn't even speak in sentences. She was marvelously healed, kind of a sovereign healing in a way. God had spoken some things to her dad. And the guy who prayed for her just said, "I bless you in Jesus' name." Then she heard the Lord tell her to anoint herself with oil. She went home and anointed herself with flaxseed oil, then she lay trembling on the floor all night. The next morning, she was normal.

**Bill:** But it was released in that meeting that you had?

**Randy:** Yes, and other mental illnesses were healed in that meeting, too. But you've actually seen more mental illnesses healed now, more manic depressives, than we have. It's amazing the breakthroughs and how they come. Didn't you say you haven't really prayed for that many?

**Bill:** We've seen close to sixty cases of bipolar being healed now, and I think we've only prayed for five or maybe six of them.

**Randy:** And the healings happen either in worship or by the testimony?

**Bill:** Yes, in worship or by the testimony. Most of them by the testimony, but some just in the worship. People will just come and say, "I heard the testimony, and I stopped taking my medicine and I'm okay." I just had somebody say that last week. It's constant.

I love the confessing of the Word you mentioned. I love how you pray what God has said in His Word over the seats for the service the next day.

**Randy:** Doing that gave me expectation. I use the word *expectation*, which is my favorite word. The word *faith* has lost its cutting edge for a lot of people. They think faith is just believing God can do something. But faith is much more than that. In some ways, faith that moves mountains is not what you *believe* God can do, it's what you *expect He's about to do*. And that's a different feeling. To me, it's not even the gift of faith. A few times in my life, fewer times than I can count on my ten fingers in forty years of ministry, I was given the gift of faith, and I knew beyond a shadow of a doubt that what I was getting ready to say was going to happen. There wasn't a bit of doubt.

I teach people in our schools that if you believe you have the gift of faith, whatever you say happens. And you can't blame the person if it didn't happen. Don't blame them and say, "Well, I have the gift of faith—but you didn't have any, so you didn't get healed." Don't do that, because if you really had the gift of faith, they could be dead and experience healing. When you have the gift of faith, it doesn't require anything on their part.

# 10

## BREAKTHROUGH INSIGHTS AND INCREASES

**Bill:** Can you trace any other major breakthroughs back to experiences and/or insights, Randy? Has there been any time that the Lord has spoken something to you out of His Word and it gave you an insight that brought an increase for healing?

**Randy:** Yes. The first instance happened about two years ago, and the second about a year ago. The first came out of 2 Corinthians 4:13, where Paul said, "It is written: 'I believed; therefore I have spoken.' With that same spirit of faith we also believe and therefore speak."

I'd seen this Scripture many times, but when God quickened it to me, all of a sudden it took on life. All of a sudden I made this connection: Faith needs to be spoken. You can say you believe something, but if you don't have enough faith to declare it, to speak it, there's something that's not released. I do not believe what the New Agers teach, that we make our reality by the words we speak. That's the difference between Christian and New Age thinking. Christian thinking is that the Lord is the one who gives the faith. We're in a dependent relationship with Him—we can't create anything we want. We create what He's *showing* us.

I realized I could speak things in faith, things that God is showing me. I used to say, "I believe God is going to heal some people tonight," but I quit saying that. I started paying attention to numbers, and over time I started connecting the dots. I'd see how many people were in attendance and then how many got healed, and God showed me a pattern. We almost never have fewer than 10 percent get healed.

**Bill:** Do you mean of total attendance?

**Randy:** Yes, of total attendance. If there were a thousand people in a service, at least one hundred would be healed. If there were one hundred attending, ten would be healed. If we had a really good meeting, it would be 20 percent healed. If we had a great meeting, it would be 30 percent. And sometimes—on our last trip, for example—100 percent were healed! In a smaller meeting, every single person they prayed for got healed. In one meeting it was 90 percent.

So it may sound bold, but based on what God has shown me, I've started speaking out the minimum number of people in a meeting who will be healed. One guy down in Brazil, Alan Hawkins, hadn't seen me for three years and noticed the difference right away. He said, "Randy, there's been a quantum leap in where you're at now compared with when I came with you three years ago. You may not see it because it's been gradual for you. But I haven't been with you for three years, and you're in another place. You say things now that you didn't used to say."

I asked him, "Like what?"

He said, "You just get up and declare, 'God is going to heal . . .' and you declare how many people."

That's true. Now when I go into a meeting, I almost always find out how many people are there, then I'll declare, "Tonight before we leave, God is going to heal . . ." and I'll say 10 percent of whatever the attendance count is. Actually, Bill, that doesn't take faith now because I am so confident in the faithfulness of God. Based on what He has shown me, we'd have to have a terrible meeting not to have at least 10 percent healed.

This is something that happened at your church the first time I came. You'll remember it. Ben was with me. The first time we came, we were there for several days. At that time, you could seat about 1,000 people. And I knew if there were 1,000 in the room, on average 30 people would get healed, approximately 30 people would get saved, and about 30 people would go through deliverance. It was something I'd been watching for over two years. So we prayed, and 25 were healed, which is close to the 30 mark. And afterward, when we prayed with the laying on of hands, we had over 30 again. And I had an impression that helped me have a major breakthrough. I wish I would have thought of this a while ago! God impressed this on me: *I want you to pray the way Abraham did for Sodom and Gomorrah.*

**Bill:** But backward?

**Randy:** Backward! Instead of the numbers going down, 50, 40, 30, 20, 10, they would go up. God impressed me, *I want you to ask Me the way Abraham did for people, but go the other way and ask Me for the number you have faith for.*

After that first one, we had 25 people healed. And I told your church, "I just felt as though God spoke to me." I asked them, "Do you think God is tired?"

"No!" they replied.

131

"Do you think He's run out of power?" I continued.

"No!" they said.

"Neither do I. Lord, I ask You for 50." That was more than we had been seeing. If I remember right, I wrote it down in my Bible that night; it's one of those memorable things you write down. And we had 57 healings.

The Lord gave me the same impression again: *Ask Me for more, according to the measure of faith you have.*

So I asked the congregation, "Do you think God is tired?"

"No!"

"Do you think He's run out of power?"

"No!"

"So let's ask Him for 75." And we prayed again and counted, and now we had a total of exactly 75 healings. Then we went for 100, and I think if I remember, if we counted them right, we had 134!

Someone in the church came up and asked me, "Why did you take so long? Why didn't you just ask God for 100 to begin with?"

I said, "You don't get it—it's not that I can just pull out a number. When we were at 25, I didn't have faith for 100, I didn't. After that, I had faith for 50 next, but not yet 75. God said, 'Pray like Abraham, and ask Me according to your measure of faith.' So that's what I did."

All throughout these years, I've continued to do that many, many times. One time a translator was helping me in the ministry. We were in a big church down in Brazil, and she had watched me do this a lot. She leaned over to me and said, "You need to ask for more."

I said, "Oh, yeah? How many do you think we ought to ask for?" We were asking for 50 or maybe 70.

She said a huge number; I don't remember whether it was 150 or 200 people, and she said it right out loud in front of everybody.

I was dumbfounded. I thought, *I don't have faith for that.* I really didn't, and I knew it, so I said, "*You* pray for that." And God gave her the faith, and she prayed and we had that many people healed. It was an amazing jump from where I had been. That time was really helpful.

**Bill:** You mentioned you had an insight from Scripture two years ago, and another one a year ago. Did we cover them both?

**Randy:** No, the other one came when I was in Brazil again, on the way to this Baptist church, Agua Vidas (Living Waters) Church. And I was thinking in my mind, *In Jesus Christ, it's not yes and no—it's yes.*

I didn't know where the Scripture reference was, but all these people had iPhones, so they took out their little Bible programs and they looked it up for me. It was 2 Corinthians chapter one. I read that passage, and verse 20 was the key: "For no matter how many promises God has made, they are 'Yes' in Christ. And so through him the 'Amen' is spoken by us to the glory of God." I had read that a lot, but all of a sudden it was as if the lights went on. These promises are not just biblical promises, though they include that. They are rhema word promises. They're not yes and no. It's not us saying, "Yes, I want it" and God saying, "If I give you a promise, sometimes it's no." It's always yes regarding His promises. They're always yes. So, I got that, but that wasn't the part that really stood out to me. It was "And so through him [enabled by the Spirit] the 'Amen' is spoken by us"—and it was a plural.

And I got an understanding that the greatest miracles we'll see in the future will come when we have taught the Church to raise their corporate faith. People need to know that if someone gets a word of knowledge for somebody else, it's just not the person giving the word whose faith goes up and who increases others' faith. The whole congregation needs to understand how God works. When they understand the ways of God, it literally causes the whole congregation to rise up in their hearts and say, "Yes, God's getting ready to do this!" So all of us speak the "Amen," which means "let it be" or "so be it," to the glory of God.

I had already had a revelation before that *glory* is a synonym for the power of God, and that the power of God is the way He glorifies His name. So for us to say the "Amen" corporately was the thing God was looking for in order to release even greater miracles that would be to His glory. I began teaching on that, and it brought life to me and helped me understand the important role of raising the faith corporately in a service.

**Bill:** One of the things that has so impacted me in your teachings on healing is how you model what you're learning when you're learning it. You put things into practice, but you don't have an ounce of hype in you. That hype thing really frightens me because it borders so closely on dishonesty, but that has no part in what you do.

I'm thinking of a specific situation I learned from when we were in Brazil. You got a mental picture, which was fairly new for you at the time, of a white van upside down and people caught with the seat belt. It was very elaborate for such a snapshot picture. But when I see you move in ways like that, it's risky in the sense that you're bringing up something that's really different for all of us. Yet you do it in such a way that when you're done, I feel as if I can do it, too. Can you talk to us about that process?

**Randy:** I remember that mental picture. That was the first one, and I wasn't sure if it was a dream or if I was awake.

**Bill:** That's bizarre. So it didn't come in the meeting?

**Randy:** No, it wasn't in the meeting; it was before we even got to the meeting. I was resting because I was exhausted—it was one of those "two naps in Brazil, one at night and one in the afternoon" kinds of trips. I honestly never figured out if I was awake when it came or if I woke up right afterward. I hadn't heard yet about words of knowledge coming through dreams. I just heard that about a year ago through some Mozambicans, and after that I had faith for it. But this time was the first time it had happened to me, then it happened in Joseph Garlington's church, as well.

Whenever I'm not sure about something, I'm careful how I phrase it. For instance, you've heard me say many times concerning angels, "*I think* God just told me angels are in the room." That's what we're supposed to do. When it came to that mental picture, I figured, *I'm not sure, and if it's God, it's going to work. If it doesn't happen, then I missed God. But the only way I'm going to know is to go for it.*

So I was really honest. I didn't get up there and say, "God just told me," and try to rev up faith by acting confident when I really wasn't. I can't do that, because if I'm wrong, that will feel worse and hurt the meeting worse than if I am just honest from the start.

I came into that meeting you're talking about and gave all the words of knowledge I was sure about first. Like always, I saved the one I was new in and learning in for last, in case it was wrong and I missed it. That way, it wouldn't do so much damage. I told the people, "*I think* I saw something, and I've got to know if it's really God or not. I don't want you to come up unless this really happened to you. You were in a vehicle, a white vehicle turned upside down, you were hanging from the seat belt and you have complications with a back problem as a result." I even knew what vertebrae it involved. I even repeated,

"I don't want you to come up here unless you really were in an accident, turned upside down and hanging by the seat belt."

Bill: And you had four people respond! How do you have four people who are in the same kind of car with such an unusual experience? Four!

Randy: And three of them were healed instantly, and the fourth just took a few minutes longer. I learned from that.

Bill: I did, too.

Randy: I don't have those mental pictures very much, but I'm getting them more than I used to. But I do process out loud, which means I explain the process I'm going through in trying to hear from God and respond faithfully to what I think He's asking me to do. I try to explain what I was thinking, what I was feeling and why I did what I did.

Bill: I think the Lord is expanding us in the mental pictures. The great evangelist and healing minister William Branham used to process out loud the way you do. He seemed to take people on a journey with him; at least it looks like it from what we've read.

Randy: And also from watching the videos of him.

Bill: He was so humble and unimpressed with himself. Going on spiritual journeys with people like him makes it possible for all of us to learn. That's the way I pick up on things from you all the time.

# 11

## THE WORSHIP
## AND THE GLORY

**Bill:** Another experience I just thought of, Randy, was when we were in the Dominican Republic together. Some healings were taking place, and then you turned the direction of the service because you felt as though we were supposed to go into worship. Connect the dots for me. I believe in the power of worship because of what we've seen. But explain here the worship element—not just the experiment on that one occasion—but the worship element in miracles. And also in that one situation, what happened?

**Randy:** That was the first time that ever happened. I'll talk more about that worship time in the Dominican Republic in a minute, but it also reminds me of the time the glory came into a room in North Carolina. That was a huge breakthrough for us. It was interesting because I had four interns going out with me for their first time, and God let them be present the first time the glory came. The first time for me—in fact, maybe the only time it was like that—these interns were there.

This insight came when I was pastoring the Vineyard church back then, and we didn't even have a building. We were still in the initial stages, meeting in a gym. We had a very powerful worship service one Sunday, in which the presence of God was so strong. On the following Monday morning, the Lord awakened me with such a loud impression—I don't think it was audible, but boy, it sure was loud. It was this: *When My presence is in your midst in worship, so is My anointing to heal the sick.* And that was it, it was over.

Several years went by, and as you said, we were in the Dominican Republic. I had spent forty-five minutes the night before in words of knowledge, and a lot of people, a couple hundred I think, had been healed. Sometimes I really don't care if I preach a short message or don't even preach at all, but this night I really felt I had a message for the pastors who were present. Because of the length of the worship we'd just had, if I went into healing words, there wouldn't be time for preaching the Word. I started praying, *Lord, I believe You want to heal, and I don't think we should allow our time limitation here to limit what You can do.* As I was trying to figure out how we could fit it all in, the Holy Spirit brought back fresh to my memory what the Lord had impressed on me years before: *When My presence is in your midst in worship, so is My power to heal.*

I remembered one song they had sung that had more anointing on it than all the others, so I announced, "I think we're supposed to sing this song, and I believe as we sing this song, God is going to heal you. We're going to sing the song, count to three and give a shout, and when we're done, I want you to check your bodies out. Then everyone who has been healed, wave at me."

I have to confess, I was scared. I thought, *I hope this is God!* Sometimes the only way to know is just to do it. But notice I didn't say, "God told me." I said, "*I think* this is what we're supposed to do." I qualified it.

We did it. We sang the song and counted to three and gave a shout. Over two hundred people got healed. It was as many as the night before, and it took only ten minutes instead of forty-five.

Now, the problem with that is the temptation to repeat it, and it's harder to do the second time than the first. You'd think it'd be easier. It's tempting the first time to think, *God may be showing me something here*, and then try it a second time because it worked the first time. But I've probably only done this kind of thing maybe ten times in the last five years. Or some variation of it, because I don't want to make it into a formula.

That last time we were down in Brazil, though, just a few weeks ago, we had the same situation come up. I had only preached five minutes the night before, and I felt I was supposed to preach a little longer, so we weren't going to have words of knowledge. I told everyone, "We're not going to have words of knowledge tonight." One guy was devastated because he just knew if there were words of knowledge, he would get healed. And instead, I did something I had done only one other time, in Santarém, Brazil. I said, "We're going to say together in unison, 'The Lord is good; His mercy endures forever,' twenty times. And then I'll count to three and we're going to give a shout, and people are going to be healed."

I felt as though we were supposed to do that, especially since we had been talking about the goodness of God. I felt this would really drive that home. That's also the time the glory came, by the way. It came a couple times, people said.

Sometimes I can't tell you why I do what I do. It may not be clear which way to go, may not be a certainty, but sometimes I have a knowing. One direction just feels more comfortable than another. It may not be a strong knowing, even. I may just say, "Let's do this . . ." to the people, and I may not even know why. So that night, we spoke together in unison, the way I directed. A doctor was present who was giving herself 80 milligrams of morphine a day for her own neck pain. She testified, "The twelfth time everyone said 'The Lord is good,' I was healed."

The guy I already mentioned said, "I was so devastated when you said there wouldn't be any words of knowledge, and you were going to do the twenty and the three and the shout. And on the twentieth time, I was healed." We had a number of healings like that, but the difficulty of that is the temptation to begin to trust in the method rather than in hearing the voice of God.

I would say one of the other big things I've learned is that for years I was missing at least half of what God was telling me. That was because I kept thinking I had to wait for very strong impressions. Only in the last three years have I lowered my level of expectation about how strong an impression has to be before I'll give it.

**Bill:** That's a good way to put it.

**Randy:** Before, an impression had to be pretty strong before I'd risk going with it. But over the last few years, I've realized that I am hearing so much more than what I thought. And sometimes I was sure I wasn't hearing God at all—then later I found out it was God. And I realized that a lot of the time in ministry, a thought that comes is from God. It may not be intensely strong, but I let it come back more than once, and I go with it. That's been helpful.

**Bill:** We just learned something like that from one of our children in the church. A couple of ministry students were ministering prophetically, and they happened to be on a team that included a small child. They soon noticed that the child nailed it every time they prayed for someone—I mean absolutely nailed it. So at the end of their time, they asked the child, "How long have you been doing this?" (We do train our grade-school children in all this.)

The boy said, "This is my first time."

The students asked him, "How is it you could do this so well?"

The boy replied, "Well, my teacher said it was my turn, so I just figured anything that came to my mind was God."

That's lowering the level! Sometimes a word or thought has to impress me really strongly before I'll take the risk and give it, and here a kid who didn't know any better just figured if it was his turn, he could say whatever came to his mind and it would be God!

Now, tell me about the glory, Randy. That's my biggest interest, when the glory shows up like that.

**Randy:** I mentioned briefly that we were in North Carolina when it first happened; I can't think of the city right now. I was preaching a sermon on open heaven and all the phenomena we were seeing in Brazil. You've heard me teach that message. But I was explaining that, in the midst of the message, a woman right in front of me, on my left and about halfway back, stood up and yelled, "Do you see it?!"

People's jaws dropped, and their eyes bugged out. And it was happening right in front of my four interns who were with me for the first time, as I said. They literally prostrated themselves.

I couldn't see anything because the spotlights were in my eyes. So I came down and looked, and I could see translucent heat waves going up, like you might see on a hot day across a plain. You can see through them, but you can also see them. It looked like that. You could see through this glory, yet still see it. It looked as if someone poured out a five-gallon bucket of finely ground silver, gold, blue, green and red substance. (I'm talking about colors; I'm not saying it was metal.) And it had an irradiance, as though light was pulsing from it, and it seemed to be spinning at different levels.

**Bill:** But it wasn't falling.

**Randy:** It wasn't falling to the ground; it was suspended. It was like looking at the Milky Way or something like a galaxy, but it was here. A couple times before, I felt as if I were almost electrocuted by God, so I made my way really carefully around it, thinking, *I don't know if I want to touch that or not.* But my curiosity got the best of me—I couldn't stand it. So I touched it and it didn't hurt, didn't electrocute me or anything. I stepped right into the middle of it—it was big enough for me to step into it. I was looking around me, and all of a sudden I just kind of lost track of everything. I thought, *Oh, man, this is the most peaceful feeling I've ever felt.* I was amazed, and I wondered if I could touch one of the particles that looked like radiating glitter. I tried to touch one, and it moved away, not letting me touch it. Then I realized, *I have no idea how long I've been in here, and I'm supposed to be leading this meeting.* So I stepped out and thought, *What do I do now?*

They don't teach you in college or seminary what to do when the glory cloud shows up. So I said, "He's here—we ought to worship Him." And I do think that was the right thing to do. We worshiped for another twenty minutes, then I remembered that when His presence is in our midst, so is His power to heal. I said, "He's here, His presence is here, so let's pray for healing again."

After we prayed for healing, I think I counted that it was two or three times the number of people who were healed on the side of the building the glory cloud rested on than on the other side. I don't want to exaggerate, but I know a lot more were healed near the glory cloud. A man who'd been deaf for fifty years was sovereignly healed. He was in the artillery in the Korean War and had been deaf ever since. No one prayed for him; he was just sitting right in front of the glory cloud. And he yelled at the pastor, "Pastor John, I can hear! I haven't been able to hear for fifty years; that's why I fall asleep on Sunday mornings when you're preaching. I don't have a clue what you're preaching; I can't hear you. My ears just opened!"

As all this was taking place, I started thinking, *Okay, now we've worshiped, we've prayed for the sick—what should we do next?* My rational mind was saying, *God came while I was talking about this message; maybe He likes it. I ought to finish it.* I think I missed it there. I've gone back over that night so many times in my mind. It's kind of like a coach looking at the game plan afterward.

**Bill:** Like watching game films.

**Randy:** Yes, game films. I thought, *Randy, you did all right on those first two directions, but that last thing, you missed it!* I'm really not trying to be falsely modest, I just honestly think I missed it. Because the cloud began to go up toward the ceiling as I was preaching. For over two hours, it never left the building. Like a thin layer of cigarette smoke in a room, it went all across the top of the stage area, near the ceiling, and stayed there during the sermon.

If you were to ask me what I would do if the glory cloud comes again, I'd tell you I'd take a different direction. I've told the Lord, "If You'll give me another chance, I know what I want to do next time." But the irony of this is, if this works, it won't work—but it will work. I'll explain that in a minute.

143

If it happens again, I'll have us worship and keep worshiping, and I'll have the people who are terminally ill line up first and step into the cloud and stay there either until they fall out or five minutes go by. Then they can step out of the cloud and let the next person step in.

When I came up with that, I thought, *Now that's going to work!* I believe people would get healed just by being in the glory. Proximity was key to some of the healings that took place the first time. After the terminally ill, then others could step in for healing. I thought about all this for a long time, and over a year later, I had to tell myself, *In some ways, that won't work as well as you think it's going to work. It's going to work so well that you're not going to know how to end the meeting!* It will be like William Branham in Arkansas, when he wasn't going to leave the stage. They didn't have cell phones or iPads or iPhones then. All they had was word of mouth, and the word got out and that line never ended until after eight days. It almost wrecked his health.

With today's technology, word would get out all over, and fast. Before you know it, people would be coming from all over the world to a meeting like that. So I realized that what I have in mind for the next time will work, but also won't work—by which I mean it's not going to just work for four hours and then we get to end the service and go home. It will go on until God sovereignly lifts it; we're not going to get to go home on our time. It will be like tending the fire. We could bring more worshipers in, and when we're exhausted we could just go lie down and let someone else tend the fire. But let's not leave; let's not let the fire go out!

**Bill:** It's a mystery to me why we're not more perceptive in those unusual moments. I had a time last year where it just started raining in the school. Actually raining indoors. We were doing question and answer time, and somebody asked me about worship and it started raining. Do you remember that time when the same thing happened in Las Vegas in the center of that stage? Paul Goulet (pastor of International Church of Las Vegas) at least had the sense to have people walk through the rain when it happened at his church. (This was during their annual Holy Spirit conference.) It rained for two or three hours. And center stage in our building, it just started raining. I didn't know what to do. I just stood there stupid. I've regretted it, and I've rehearsed what to do next time.

**Randy:** Did you tell the Lord, "Give me another chance," the way I did?

**Bill:** Yeah, give me another one. I don't know what I'll do, but it will be different than just standing there! I guess I don't have an answer . . . you can't be an expert on something you've never heard of or experienced. The Lord knows I'm a rookie, and He knows I don't know what I'm doing. How can I be more perceptive in that moment?

I like your thoughts about healing in those moments, and getting people thinking redemptively of a manifestation. God never shows up to entertain. He's always redemptive.

**Randy:** Right. He doesn't show up or give a word to tease. A word is a promise.

**Bill:** True. I don't want to manipulate or use those moments, but we at least should immediately start thinking redemptively just because of who He is. I like that; I can work with that. Jesus, help me.

# 12

# LEARNING TO FOLLOW
# GOD'S LEAD

**Bill:** What about learning to hear from God better, Randy? What experiences or insights have you had that have taught you how to hear Him or have helped you learn to follow His lead? What kinds of experiences have really accelerated your growth?

**Randy:** When I first got words of knowledge I was 32, I was a Baptist pastor and I had no pains in my body. So if I got a word of knowledge, if I felt it in my body, I was 90 percent accurate from day one. If I had an impression, it was only maybe 25 percent accurate. After about the first three weeks, I shut the impressions down. I leaned toward my strength, feeling the words, instead.

I wouldn't risk giving the impressions when I had a 75 percent chance of being wrong, so I didn't develop that. I just never would go for impressions, especially subtle ones. I didn't have any confidence unless an impression was very, very strong and kept coming.

When I began to get older, in my fifties, I discovered something new. I don't mean to say this to get people to laugh—I'm dead serious about it. I realized that the older I get, the more my own pain can contaminate what I'm feeling and cause me to be wrong. When I'm getting a word, it's not my own pain I feel, it's a sympathetic pain. I don't have whatever's causing it. But the older you get, the more pains you start having. In my case, that meant the more that 90 percent accuracy rate could start going down when it comes to words I feel. In light of that, I told the Lord, "Lord, I'm sorry I shut this other area of impressions down. I need it to be resurrected; I need to grow in it."

When I first intentionally decided I wanted to start going for impressions, I was leery. But I asked the Lord for them and told Him I'd start going for them. At that point, I had never gotten a mental picture as a word. People in my first church used to have so many of those that it amazed me. I was always amazed by the seer. And Bob Jones had told me, "God wants you to see. You do see. An impression is seeing—it's perceiving."

Ruth Heflin had said, "God wants you to see." Over and over I got several prophecies from Ruth Heflin regarding the idea, "God wants you to see."

One of the first times I got an impression as a mental picture was in Joseph Garlington's church in Pittsburgh. I felt a pain and got an impression that it was from an accident. I could have just said that, because I believe the more information you have, the more faith it creates. I could have told the people exactly what vertebrae, where it was and what it felt like. That's different from saying, "You have back pain." I can tell you more details about where a pain is and how it feels because they all don't feel the same to me. They feel very different.

Then I got an impression that this pain was the result of a car accident. I got this word before the service started, so I wrote it down—where it was in the back so I'd remember how it felt, and that it was from an accident. I actually wrote down "Possibly an accident," and I drew a little dotted line around it. That's the way I teach myself. I circled it and put a question mark outside it or something. Then for a split second, I thought I saw a green Jeep Cherokee. It wasn't wrecked; I just saw it. So I drew another line out from what I first wrote and put "Green Jeep Cherokee" in a circle with another question mark.

In my thinking process, I normally start from where I'm at, so I had decided to say, "I think there's somebody here with a problem in this vertebrae," and then say, "and it's from an accident." If I got those right, I would risk it and say, "I think you were driving a green Jeep Cherokee." But it was so subtle, *so* subtle. Just that split-second image. I prayed, *Lord, I would never have thought this was You before, but I'm going to start paying attention to the more subtle thoughts.*

So I got up and said, "I believe somebody here had an accident," and I pointed to my back and told them how it felt. I added, "It's from a car accident."

This guy jumps up and says, "That's my daughter!" (I think he said his daughter, or maybe his niece.) He went on, "She was hurt recently. She got in a wreck driving this green Jeep Cherokee."

I actually grabbed my paper and came down off the stage and showed the guy. I said, "Look, look! I was going to say green Jeep Cherokee next!"

I did hear, and I learned. Even by writing it down like that, even though I didn't get to say it, I learned. And I thought, *Oh, it would have been so much better to have gone ahead and said it to build more faith.* But the girl got healed anyway.

149

The mental picture I saw that really began to give me faith took place with Heidi Baker in southern Mozambique. Heidi had just preached and people were prostrated on the floor, seeking God. I was looking for a place to lie down, but there was nowhere. The place was just covered. I figured if I couldn't lie down, I'd lean against the wall, so I did that. I was praying because it was my first trip to Mozambique—I had just traveled halfway around the world—and my first experience was pretty bad. I wasn't connecting with the people. I like stories, but I realized I couldn't use a lot of my favorite illustrations. You can't use anything that deals with electricity, for example, because they don't have any modern conveniences and can't relate to that kind of story. So I was struggling with making a connection.

This was maybe ten years ago, but I still remember it as clear as day. I prayed, "Lord, I didn't come halfway around the world to give a teaching. These people can preach in their own language. They can teach themselves; they understand their culture. They can preach and teach here better than I can. I didn't come here to give a teaching; I came here to give what *You* want to give." And I believed for impartation. I knew God was going to use me for impartation.

Yet it was intimidating. My three translators, who worked in three different languages, all had raised the dead! I thought, *What am I even doing here when all your translators have raised the dead?* But leaning up against the wall, I prayed, "Lord, I need a word from You. Lord, I want to see something—let me see something. God, others have said I'm supposed to see, but I don't see. Why can't I see? *God, I want to see.*"

All of a sudden, I had this lightning-fast impression, then it was over. I thought, *Whoa, what was that?*

**Bill:** Did you want God to bring it back?

**Randy:** *Please*, bring it back! It wasn't like the open visions some of our friends get—that's intimidating when your friends get open visions. I feel as if my impression was so weak compared to that. So this experience was a big lesson for me. God didn't bring it back, but in that split second as I thought about it, it was as if some people were on a mountain, and they were asking God if they were to go into a new region and open that region up. They wanted to know if they could go there. They were on a mountain when this happened.

The impression unpacked a little bit for me, like a zip file on a computer. It was a lot of information for just a split-second thing. But it was so weak that I didn't know if it was God. I don't want to overuse the word, but it was weak! I wasn't sure of what I saw, and I had been so busy conversing on my way there that I hadn't even noticed if there *were* any mountains around. On the way in, I wasn't looking around; Heidi and I were talking.

The impression came to me in a meeting just after Heidi had finished speaking, while we were in a time of worship. During the dinner break after that, Pastor Surprise "Supressa" Sithole was walking with me to my first interview with someone. Supressa is very prophetic; Rolland Baker said Supressa is the most prophetic guy he's ever met. The man gets open visions like movies—and now he's raised the dead! Anyway, I asked him, "Supressa, do you get visions?"

"Yeah, I get visions," he told me.

"If you were to get a vision and I were in front of you, would you see me, or would you just see the vision?" I asked.

He said, "I wouldn't see you; I'd just see the vision. It's open vision."

"That's what I thought. I thought you got stuff like that," I said. Then I added, "Supressa, I think I might have seen something." I told him what it was, and he didn't say a word. So I went and interviewed Johnny, who had raised a woman from the dead. Then we came back and it was my turn to speak. At the end of the meeting, I said, "I need to know if this was God or not," and I gave my impression. I watered it down a little bit. I should have said, "If you were on a mountain overlooking a region, and you were asking God, 'Can I go in there and start churches?' then I want you to come up. I want to pray for you, because the answer is yes." But I didn't say only that; I added, "Or you dreamed it." I expanded it a little bit, which I shouldn't have done.

Next I was blown away! Supressa himself was weeping and trembling. "Why didn't you say something earlier when I told you?" I asked him.

"I was so shocked!" he told me. He had been asking God up on a mountain about a certain area and whether he could go into it.

Two other guys also had been on a mountain, and they had been asking God for overseers who were more experienced and grounded in the faith than they were. They went into a vision on the mountain, and it showed that they would find the overseers in this town, Chimoio. They also saw a building, and a ball of fire went over the building. It was like a half a day's walk away, yet they saw two thousand people there and fire coming down on their heads. They came the next day to tell Heidi all about it, and they came up for prayer that night, too. (Rolland and Heidi became the overseers the vision talked about.) Then these guys helped go in and pioneer that area.

On top of all that, a man named William at New Missions had been up on a mountain asking direction of God, and he got confirmation. (He had just been appointed over New Missions, the mission expansion of Iris Ministries, which is the Bakers' ministry.) So these four people really got blasted by my impression.

Later I said to Supressa, "I don't understand—that was one of the most powerful impartations in these meetings. Heidi had been praying for two months that God would show her whom to send into these two provinces, Nampula and Cabo Delgado."And I said the same thing to Heidi: "I don't understand it; it was so weak."

Supressa talked to me after that. He said, "Randy, which takes the most faith to speak? When you have an open vision, or when you have a very weak mental picture?"

"I guess it would take more faith to speak the weaker one," I said.

"Don't judge how powerful a word is going to be by how it comes," he said. "Sometimes what seems very weak can be very powerful."

Afterward, on Toronto's webpage (www.ctftoronto.com), my impression was called "The Mountain Vision." But when it came to me, I was thinking more like, *I think I might have seen something.* And as I said, I even told the people, "You might have dreamed it"—I watered it down. But still God honored it. That was a real breakthrough for me. I learned so much. Before, my mindset had been that the powerful things were more like open visions. I learned that that's not always true.

**Bill:** Here's what stands out to me. You read about Branham and some of these folks with open visions. It's a sovereign invasion, in a nice way, of God putting Himself on them. For you, though, what does your hunger for more have to do with your experience? It doesn't seem like an invasive thing for you, though God certainly can do that. But sometimes it's as if God puts something out there, and He lets us kind of figure it out and learn from it. Can you explain that connection to me?

**Randy:** There is a connection. I think of how I heard you talk about healings having to do with metal in the body, and I thought, *I want that, too.* I want to enter into the area of metal healings. I didn't have a word of knowledge. All I had was your testimony and a desire to enter into it. Those are what led me, and it happened. With my desire to see creative miracles, the hunger was so strong that it led me into the fast. We got a breakthrough there. The desire to see a breakthrough in mental illness came similarly. It wasn't by way of a testimony of Jesus; it wasn't by way of a fast. I always told the Lord, "Lord, I understand fasting doesn't twist Your arm; it doesn't gain me brownie points. I just want it to help me to focus. I say in my heart, *I want this to focus my prayer, my intensity for a breakthrough in this area.*" I even prayed, "God, Your Word says . . . Based on Your promises, I believe You want to take us into this area." A lot of breakthrough has happened that way—through desiring to grow and focusing on how, even in areas where God isn't moving invasively.

The desire to grow caused me to go to other countries early on. I knew I was growing so much in Latin America, for example, and when I'd come back, my faith level would be so much higher than when I left. So I intentionally made sure I went, and I tried to be in a place where that would happen at least a couple times a year in those early years. Now I go a lot.

**Bill:** It seems to me that the sovereign stuff is quite frankly the most exciting, when God just imposes Himself. But I feel that there's something about this pursuit of these other areas that honors Him more. It feels like that to me, anyway. We're to earnestly desire spiritual gifts. (See 1 Corinthians 14:1.) It's like these areas are there for us and need to be acknowledged, valued and run after. I know you've had some sovereign things happen where God has just presented Himself. But as I've watched in the years I've known you, so much of it is you knocking on the door. It's you saying, "I'm going to use this testimony as a springboard into something else."

Seeing that kind of stuff gives me hope, too, that I could move in those areas because I could knock down the door. I've never had any of those big encounters or experiences, either, so I've discounted myself the same way you did. Like you, I always thought you had to have a vision of God or something.

# 13

## SPECTACULAR STORIES

**Bill:** Tell us, Randy, about four or five of the greatest miracles you've seen.

**Randy:** This is one of the greatest, and it just happened a few weeks ago, when I was in Brazil. This young man in his twenties had an aneurysm. They operated, but it went wrong. I don't know if it burst while they were operating or exactly what happened, but he lost 90 percent of his hearing and his left side was paralyzed. I didn't notice it at first, but then I saw his left arm was hanging there, not moving. I touched his arm and asked, "Is there anything wrong with your arm?"

He said, "I'm paralyzed." And he pulled it up and said, "I can pull it up and I can hold it like that, but after a while it'll fall down." He also dragged his left leg.

We began praying for him, but nothing was happening. I prayed blessing on him, and I started the interview process by asking, "Are you feeling anything?"

He said, "Yeah."

"Where?"

"In my arm."

I start praying for his arm, and then I asked, "What's happening?"

"It hurts."

"What do you mean it hurts? Where does it hurt?"

He said, "It hurts where this bicep muscle ties into my elbow."

Up to this point with him, I was just trying to be faithful, praying, *God, You know what he needs.* But I didn't have strong faith that he would get healed. I hoped it and I expected that he could; I prayed for it and wanted it. But it's not like I had a gift of faith for it. Earlier that night, though, I had given a word of knowledge because I felt significant pain where the bicep muscle ties into the elbow. So as soon as he told me where it hurt, I told him, "You're going to be healed!"

I kept praying, and you could feel the heat on him. His hand was cold because of poor circulation, and you could touch his pant leg and feel how cold his leg was through the pants.

"Heat is coming down my arm," he said.

We kept praying and blessing, and to make a long story short, by the end of the night he had his hearing back. He could hear me talk from a hundred feet away. By the end of the night, he had full range of motion with his arm, and he could walk. It was a major, major healing.

Another major healing involved a woman in Odessa, Ukraine. It was one of the few times and one of the first times I had a mental picture. I saw a tractor pulling a sickle-like attachment that cut hay. I grew up on a farm; I should know what those are called! This one was folded up to go down the road. In this mental picture, a split-second one again but clear, I saw the blade fall down. The driver didn't know it fell. When he drove around a curve, the blade clipped a person at the knees and almost cut the person's legs off. (I didn't know if the person was a man or a woman). The legs weren't severed completely, but the damage was really severe.

When I saw the picture, I thought, *Oh no, Lord, I really wish I were out on a farm commune; that would be better.* I didn't see how the picture would apply to someone in a big city. I saved it for last because I had never had a word come quite like this before. I didn't know if it was God or not. I spoke it out near the end of the service, and the moment I spoke it out, I didn't even have time to pray before a woman in the back responded. She was in her sixties, but had been injured as a teenager in exactly the way I described. She'd been walking beside the road in a farm commune, when a tractor came along with the sickle falling down and cut her at the knees. It severed her tendons, almost cutting her legs off. She had not been able to walk normally since. She even had to back up stairs stiff-legged because her knees wouldn't bend. Instantly, her legs were healed. It was an instant creative miracle. That was one of the biggest, greatest miracles I have ever seen. (She was able to walk and climb stairs normally.)

**Bill:** Did anyone pray for her, or was it just the word?

**Randy:** No, no prayer at all. She was instantly healed.

Another creative miracle took place in that same church, in that same meeting. I prayed for a fourteen-year-old boy who was completely deaf in his left ear. Our teams see about two hundred deaf ears opened a year and about the same number of blind eyes opened. I may pray for a handful of those, but mostly it's the team, or sometimes just a word of knowledge.

This time, however, I was praying for this boy, and he got healed. His mother wept, she was so excited. I was thankful, but not terribly excited because we've seen quite a bit of deafness get healed. I wasn't jumping or twirling or that kind of thing. But I said to her, "Wow, this is awesome! Your boy got healed."

She said, "No, you don't understand! He doesn't have an auditory nerve. He had a high fever, and it destroyed his nerve. I took him to a specialist here and to an auditory specialist in Venice. Both confirmed that he doesn't have an auditory nerve!"

So this was a creative miracle, one of the first creative miracles I'd seen. God created an auditory nerve for that boy.

Those healings come to mind, but so many other amazing things have happened!

**Bill:** What about the guy who had no movement from his shoulders down? He also had no faith at all—his sons brought him up.

**Randy:** He didn't have any faith, yet he got healed. We don't show that one anymore because when we went back this year, we found out his healing only lasted three or four months and then the MS came back and he couldn't move anything but his eyes. But one of my board members got a team together and they went to pray for this guy again. One of his sons was so discouraged; he didn't want to go through that roller-coaster thing again with his dad. But his dad's condition was awful; the guy couldn't move anything but his eyes. The team prayed for about an hour, and then he could lift his feet off the bed again. I would say that was one of the greatest miracles; it wasn't with me, but with one of my teams.

Another of the greatest miracles we've seen also happened with one of my teams. The night it happened, I did have a woman get healed who was blind, but this is a better story. This blind man had only heavy white scar tissue where his corneas and pupils used to be. An acid spill had burned those parts of his eyes when he was a boy. This woman on our team felt led to pray for him. The service was five hours long, and she prayed for that one man the whole time. He never felt a thing; there was never any indication of anything happening. This had to be a real gift of God to give her the knowledge to do that. She left not knowing if anything had happened.

The next day there was no change in the man's eyes, and the day after that, still nothing. He went to bed blind the second night, but on the third morning after we left, he woke up with no scar tissue, brand-new eyes and perfect vision! And the doctors couldn't comprehend it because they had all his records on file.

The pastor where we had been called us and said, "It's the greatest miracle in the history of the city. All the evidence is here."

The doctors even called us two or three times for an explanation. "Tell us again how it is he can see," they would say.

I would say that was one of the greatest miracles that we've seen. I'm trying to think of some other creative miracles, too. I've got three in my head, but let me tell you about one early on in renewal that wasn't the greatest, but touched me deeply. This girl not even twenty years old was dying in a hospital. She was a dancer, and a woman in Manaus, Brazil, felt that the Lord said, *Take her dance outfit.*

The girl had this rare disease that caused sores all over, and she was in intensive care. You can't walk in and visit the patients there; it's kind of quarantined. This woman had to put a mask on and all this stuff before she could go in and see her. But this woman felt that the Lord said, *Take the girl's dance outfit to Randy and let him pray over it. Then take it to her and let them put that dance outfit on her, and I'll heal her.*

I prayed over the outfit, and then I forgot about it. I didn't remember anything. Later, this woman came up to me in another city and told me the story. She said, "That's the girl up there dancing. The moment we put the outfit on her, she was healed and began to get strong. It killed the disease right then."

You know the next story, about Susan Starr. In March this year, she was in hospice dying. Her autonomic nervous system was failing, and she would pass out multiple times a day. She took 45 pills a day, too, and suffered 10 to 15 bouts of diarrhea. She could eat almost nothing. Somehow she heard my name while she was recovering from yet another surgery. (In fact, Susan says God gave her my name even before she woke up after surgery!) She thought, *He's the one who needs to pray for me.* She came to our meeting, and it ended up that Rodney Hogue prayed for her and she got totally, instantly healed. She had so much wrong with her, so much shut down in her body. It was an amazing miracle.

One more story: Back at the Baptist church in 1984, when I was 32 years old, I was seeking God, and I was so tired of praying, "God, just guide the surgeon's hand." I thought, *There's got to be more to it than this.* Then a young lady named Tammy Ferguson came up for healing. John Gordon and I prayed for her, and her crossed eyes got healed. But we didn't know until the next night that she had spina bifida and had no control of her bladder. She was also hydrocephalic and had already undergone twelve surgeries to put in shunts. This was our first real healing—within 12 to 24 hours of our receiving anointing, she got healed of her spina bifida, she had control of her bladder and the spine now had fluid coming from the brain. She never had had that before. She never had to have another surgery, either, which again was an amazing story of healing. That really encouraged us.

**Bill:** It's amazing to me how, when you start seeing miracles, the Lord doesn't necessarily start with the common cold. In fact,

I've told people lately that I've seen more cancer healed than colds. It's not like you progress from simple diseases to serious ones. The Lord can start you in healings with really crazy serious ones. I see it often.

**Randy:** That's true. That reminds me, lately we've had several people healed of terminal cancer. The doctors had opened them up, closed them and said there's no hope—gave them less than a month to live. And just in the last year, eight or ten people in that terminal condition have been healed.

Here's a great thing. This guy from North Carolina had been saved, but he was a recovering alcoholic. His wife was a nurse and had come with us to Brazil and had seen lots of healings, so now he wanted to come on a trip, too. For two years in a row, he was as sober as can be—until right before the trip he was scheduled to go on. He got drunk and disqualified himself, and he didn't come. The third year, he finally made it on the trip. He was a contractor, a builder, and he had never prayed for anybody. But he came along because he wanted to pray for the sick and see somebody get healed.

This took place late one night after we got in, and he hadn't had any sleep for two days because he missed a flight and ended up in the airport all night. It was almost midnight and he was sleepy, but I said, "Now the team's going to pray."

The guy said this prayer: "Lord, You know I've never prayed for anybody in my life. I've never seen anybody healed. I've never even prayed for healing, so this is my first time. Bring me an easy one. A headache or a bellyache."

He looked out and here came this young man in a wheelchair, rolling toward him. Our guy goes, "No, God, not that, not that! Lord, I need an easy one. A headache or a bellyache!" And the young man rolled right up to him and pulled on his pant leg.

163

"I started to pray," he told us later. "I had read your materials about how to pray, so I interviewed the guy and there was nothing happening. My little bit of faith was gone—I knew nothing was going to happen. But I remembered you said you don't hold us responsible to heal, God heals. But you hold us responsible to love. And I felt like, *I've prayed such a short time that if I walk away right now, he'll feel rejected, not loved. So I'm going to pray longer, not in any faith that God's going to heal him, but just so he'll feel loved.*

Standing behind the wheelchair, he had one hand on his front side and the other on the guy's back. Praying from behind, he was getting sleepy. He said, "The longer I prayed, the more my head drooped on his shoulder. I was about to start snoring, when suddenly the guy jumped out of the wheelchair and hugged me and wet my shoulder with his tears!"

Now the amazing thing was why the young man was in the wheelchair. As our guy interviewed him, he found out that the man was a 25-year-old police officer who had been shot. The bullet had gone through his stomach and severed his spinal cord. The doctors told him, "You'll never walk again; you'll be a paraplegic for the rest of your life." God had to regenerate his spinal cord, and that was our guy's first miracle. His first one! As you said, God doesn't always start off with healing a cold.

**Bill:** You know, that's a big deal for people to learn, because in our human reasoning we figure that we'll start with something simple and progress. It doesn't work that way.

How about giving us a deliverance story? Do you have any great ones? I'm thinking of one of the trips to Brazil, where there was the lady that people had tried to help for years. . . .

**Randy:** Big Bertha! We were up in Belem, Brazil, when we saw her for the first time in a Quadrangular church, which in the U.S.

would be a Foursquare. Big Bertha has a reputation for trying to ruin meetings. The pastor's up there, and they're trying to cast this demon out of her. They've got hold of her and they're shaking her. One person would throw her to the next, and that person would shake her, too. They'd pull her head back and open her mouth and try to pour water down her throat. It was terrible. The people on my team were so affected. They couldn't believe this stuff was really being done to the poor woman! We've been trained in a more gentle, pastoral way.

Their camera people had the camera on the whole thing, too, so all 25,000 people could see what was going on. I was shocked; it was the first time I'd ever met this pastor, and we had arrived late, just in time to get up on the platform. Big Bertha—and she was *big*—was terrorizing the pastor, but they couldn't get the demon out. Later, we went back for this even bigger crusade, and Big Bertha showed up. Tom Hauser (one of my U.S. pastoral advisors) ministered to her and set her free. You talk about somebody who has respect among the Foursquare of Belem! I didn't see what took place that time; I just know she got free.

I saw another deliverance that was bizarre. It involved a young woman who had been a prostitute. She had come to the Lord and gotten saved, but was very demonized. She fell to the ground, contorted. Her hands were going every which way and blood was coming out of her mouth, or maybe her nose and mouth. It took a while, but seeing her set free was really powerful. (Tom Hauser was the one who ministered to her.)

Probably the most amazing deliverances I've seen were the first two that happened in my Baptist church. Classic stuff—voice changes, facial feature changes, forehead and neck swollen up. One young woman was beating her head on the floor. We didn't know what to do, but once we found out how to deal with deliverances, we were successful (nine demons cast out in two days).

165

The girl's cousin was even worse. She was 39 and used a walker. She was eaten up with arthritis, was losing her sight and was having grand mal seizures. They said she had brain damage. The last two times the girl we had already delivered went to pray for this cousin, the cousin fell out and went into grand mal seizures both times. The first time, I said, "Let's not think we have a demon under every bush. It could have been a coincidence. If you go back and it happens again, then we need to minister to her."

I only had this one girl's deliverance under my belt, and I wasn't wild about the thought of another one. I don't like deliverance anyway; I like doing other things better. But one man at the church, John, loves it now. Bill, you know John. He was awakened the night before we met this cousin; he was suffocating as if there were a hand on his throat, choking him. His room was filled with fear, just fear everywhere. And he was trying to say "Jesus," but he couldn't get the word out. Finally, at the moment he was able to say "Jesus," *bam*, the hand lifts, the fear leaves and he goes into an open vision. This vision was key to getting this cousin free. He saw her when she was 16—this is 23 years earlier—and he saw the name of the town in Illinois where she was. They have these green signs with the name of towns on them, so he read the name, then he saw the car the girl was in and knew the man who was raping her was named Mike.

We started to do the deliverance, and we were just praying when she fell out into this grand mal seizure. John went over and said, "I know all about you; you tried to kill me last night." The Lord had given him two names of the spirits that were in her, so he called them out. Things were getting so weird that I thought maybe it was just a coincidence, but when he called them out, the swinging doors at the back of the church creaked.

It was like the *Twilight Zone*. It was only the second deliverance
I had ever seen, and it was the most classic of all.

Then John told her he also had heard the word *adultery*.

"It wasn't me, it wasn't me," she said.

John said, "Yes, it was. God told me. I heard the word *adultery*."
Then she got angry. She said, "It was my husband—I caught
him two weeks ago in the garage with a young girl. I wanted to
shoot him with a shotgun."

"Oh, forgive me, forgive me!" John said right away. "I thought
it was you." John learned a lot that day. But all the stuff God
was showing John was true and he kept going with her, and in a
classic deliverance she got free. I took her through inner healing
after that. John would say to me, "I got the demons out—you
do the inner healing part!"

To this day, I still don't really like deliverance. It takes longer,
and I like the healing and impartation ministry. So when we do
crusades, we take some people along who really do well with
deliverance, and we'll usually have a deliverance tent, a healing
tent and then a tent for the critically ill. All during services,
they'll have circles of people praying for the critically ill. I want
to do those in the United States one day.

**Bill:** How often, Randy, do you see a connection between the
demonic and a healing? (We have asked each other this question
on a regular basis. Each time we do, our conclusion is that the
demonic is even more involved than we thought the previous
time we asked it.)

**Randy:** More of a connection than I used to think. You and I,
along with other leaders in the Revival Alliance, started talking
about this about ten years ago. And still, every time you and I
talk about it, I say, "There's more of a connection than what
I thought."

In Brazil, there's more of a connection than here in the U.S. because there's so much witchcraft in Brazil and so many people go to spiritualists. But as New Age belief becomes stronger here, I believe we'll see more and more people sick in America. Going to Reiki and this type of thing, I believe people are opening themselves up to the demonic. I think we'll begin to see the effects of that.

Sometimes 25 percent of the sicknesses we see are connected to the demonic; sometimes it's more. It's not like the percentage is consistent. The connection is stronger in certain places than in others, as I said. But to say that there are no afflicting spirits at the root of sickness is just as wrong as to say that every sickness is caused by a spirit. With a lot of the classic early Pentecostal healers, pretty much everything was seen as demonic somehow. It was just where they were at back then. But I don't think that's true—and neither do I think it's true that it's never.

**Bill:** Amazing. This whole time has been good. Thanks for taking the time. I love to hear your stories, and listening to your perspective helps me so much. I think putting this kind of information on film and in writing will be helpful to so many people long-term. Thanks for doing it.

**Randy:** I think so, too. If people can watch these interviews on DVD or read this book and gain insight and understanding about the spiritual principles involved in healing, that will help them to help others. Thank you for being part of this, Bill.

**Bill Johnson** is a fifth-generation pastor with a rich heritage in the Holy Spirit. Together, Bill and his wife, Beni, serve as the senior pastors of Bethel Church in Redding, California. They also serve a growing number of churches that have partnered for revival. This leadership network has crossed denominational lines, building relationships that enable church leaders to walk successfully in both purity and power.

The present move of God has brought Bill into a deeper understanding of the phrase "on earth as it is in heaven." Jesus lived out this principle by doing only what He saw His Father doing. Heaven was the model for Jesus' life and ministry—and Bill makes it his model, as well. Bill demonstrates how recognizing the Holy Spirit's presence and following His lead enables believers to do the works of Christ, destroying the works of the devil.

Bill and his church family regularly see healings in areas ranging from cancer to broken bones to learning disorders to emotional trauma. These works of God are not limited to revival meetings or church services. Bill teaches that believers need to take this anointing into schools, the workplace and their neighborhoods with similar results. We owe the world an encounter with God, he says, and a gospel without power is not the Gospel that Jesus preached. Bill believes that healing and deliverance must become the common expression of this Gospel of power once again.

Bill and Beni have three children and nine wonderful grandchildren. All three of their children are married and involved in full-time ministry with their spouses. To learn more about Bill Johnson, his ministry and his resource materials, visit www .ibethel.org and www.bjm.org.

## Other Books by Bill Johnson

*The Center of the Universe*

*Dreaming with God*

*The Essential Guide to Healing* (co-authored with Randy Clark)

*Experience the Impossible*

*Face to Face with God*

*The Power That Changes the World*

*Release the Power of Jesus*

*Strengthen Yourself in the Lord*

*The Supernatural Power of a Transformed Mind*

*When Heaven Invades Earth*

**Randy Clark** is best known for helping spark the move of God now affectionately labeled "the Toronto Blessing." In the years since, his influence has grown as an international speaker. He continues, with great tenacity, to demonstrate the Lord's power to heal the sick.

Randy received his M.Div. from The Southern Baptist Theological Seminary, and he is presently working on his D.Min. from United Theological Seminary (Dayton, Ohio). His message is simple: "God wants to use you." He has written or helped compile eight books, including *There Is More*, sixteen booklets and four workbooks or training manuals.

The most important aspect of his calling to ministry is the way God uses him for impartation. In January 1984, John Wimber heard God speak audibly the first two times he met Randy, telling John that Randy would one day go around the world laying his hands on pastors and leaders for the impartation and activation of the gifts of the Holy Spirit. In January 1994, in the early days of the outpouring of the Spirit in Toronto, John called Randy and told him that what God had shown him about Randy was beginning now. It has continued ever since.

Randy has the unique ability to minister to many denominations and apostolic networks. These have included Roman Catholics, Messianic Jews, Methodists, many Pentecostal and charismatic congregations, and the largest Baptist churches in Argentina, Brazil and South Africa. He has also taken several thousand people with him on international ministry teams. His co-author, Bill Johnson, says the fastest way to increase in the supernatural is to accompany Randy on an international trip. Randy has traveled to over forty countries and continues to travel extensively to see that God's mandate on his life is fulfilled. He also serves a network of churches and itinerant ministries.

Randy and his wife, DeAnne, reside in Mechanicsburg, Pennsylvania. They have four adult children, three of whom are married, and two grandchildren. For more information about Randy Clark, his ministry and his resource materials, visit www .globalawakening.com.

## Other Books by Randy Clark

*The Biblical Guidebook to Deliverance*

*Changed in a Moment*

*Entertaining Angels*

*The Essential Guide to Healing* (book and curriculum kit, with co-author Bill Johnson)

*The Essential Guide to the Power of the Holy Spirit*

*Finding Victory When Healing Doesn't Happen* (with Craig Miller)

*Healing Energy: Whose Is It?* (with Susan Thompson)

*Healing Is in the Atonement: The Power of the Lord's Supper*

*The Healing River and Its Contributing Streams*

*Lighting Fires*

*Power, Holiness and Evangelism*

*Supernatural Missions*

*There Is More!*

## Booklets

*Awed by His Grace/Out of the Bunkhouse*

*Baptism in the Holy Spirit*

*Biblical Basis for Healing*

*Christ in You, the Hope of Glory*

*Evangelism Unleashed*

*Falling Under the Power of the Holy Spirit*

*Healing Out of Intimacy/Acts of Obedience*

*Learning to Minister under the Anointing/Healing Ministry in Your Church*

*Open Heaven/Are You Thirsty?*

*Pressing In/Spend and Be Spent*

*The Thrill of Victory/The Agony of Defeat*

*Words of Knowledge*

## Ministry Materials

*Ministry Team Training Manual*

*School of Healing and Impartation (SHI) Workbooks:*

*SHI Kingdom Foundations (Revival Phenomena and Healing)*

*SHI Healing: Spiritual and Medical Perspectives*

*SHI Empowered (Deliverance, Disbelief, and Deception)*